Yuletide Jollies

Geza Tatrallyay

ISBN: 978-93-6354-062-0

First Edition: 2024
Rs. 200/- USD 15.00

Cyberwit.net
HIG 45 Kaushambi Kunj, Kalindipuram
Allahabad - 211011 (U.P.) India
http://www.cyberwit.net
Tel: +(91) 9415091004
E-mail: info@cyberwit.net

Printed at Repro India Limited.

For my parents, Peter and Lily, and my wonderful wife, Marcia, without whom our Christmas celebrations each year would not have been so much fun.

Acknowledgements

As this is a compilation of some new and previous works I wrote on the subject of Christmas, I would like to acknowledge those that were published in my other books:

For the Children was previously published by Editions Dedicaces in 2015, with a new edition and ebook version by Ingram in April 2024. Its **Chapters 13** to **16** are republished here as **Our First Christmas in the Free West**.

Pathétique, or Famine in Ethiopia Viewed on St. Nicholas' Day was previously published in my second poetry collection, ***Sighs and Murmurs***, by P.R.A. Publishing in 2018.

The Expo Affair was published under their MiroLand Imprint by Guernica Editions in 2016. The beginning of its **Chapter 1** is included here as **An Unexpected Christmas Gift.**

Christmas and afterthoughts was previously published in my second poetry collection, ***Sighs and Murmurs,*** by P.R.A. Publishing in 2018.

Christmas Eve twenty-twenty was previously published in my fifth poetry collection, ***The Abyss,*** by Deux Voiliers Publishing in 2022.

Opi and the Sidecar Christmas was previously published in my short story collection, ***The Mind Spins,*** by P.R.A. Publishing in 2021.

The Nutcracker was previously published in my fourth poetry collection ***Extinction Rebellion,*** by Cyberwit.net in 2020.

Twisted Fates, the third book in my 'Twisted' trilogy of thrillers, was published by Black Opal Books in 2018. It is the **Epilogue** that is included here as **Christmas in Vermont.**

Let's ring in the New Year was previously published in my fifth poetry collection, ***The Abyss,*** by Deux Voiliers Publishing in 2022.

Contents

Foreword

Christmas has always been my favorite holiday. As a non-believer, not so much for what it is meant to celebrate in our western, Christian cultures – the birth of Jesus Christ, the savior – nor for the usual exchange of gifts, but rather for all the mystery and magic, all the wonderful stories associated with the holiday month: Santa Claus or Saint Nicholas, yes, even the birth of Jesus in a manger in Bethlehem, the Three Kings and their gifts of gold, frankincense and myrrh, Rudolf the Red-Nosed Reindeer, the Norse and Old Germanic Yule, or rebirth of the sun, the Roman orgiastic festival of Saturnalia honoring their god of agriculture and so on.

Christmastime was also seminal in shaping me as an individual: our escape from Stalinist Hungary in 1956 and emigration as refugees to Canada culminated right around the holiday. So, as an aging adult, now I relish more the togetherness with loved ones, old and young, the evoking of memories of past Christmases and of those no longer with us, the tradition filled celebrations, and of course – I, the glutton, must admit – the delicious meals and wonderful wines and champagne that are served *de rigueur* over the few days of the holidays. For us, the feasting has come to be extended by a number of birthdays that happen to fall at the end of December, which bring yet another special meaning to the season.

My love of this particular holiday time and all that goes with it has come to be reflected in my writing over the years. I have written about it in my memoirs, thrillers, short stories, and poetry, and even tried my hand at a Christmastime children's story. I thought it would be fun to collect all of these instances where Christmas and its accompanying festivities have been featured in my various books into one little multi-genre volume, and *Yuletide Jollies* is the result. I hope you, my reader, derive as much pleasure reading it, as I did compiling it, and of course, writing the original pieces.

Geza Tatrallyay
Barnard, Vermont

Our First Christmas in the Free West

This selection is an excerpt from my first memoir, ***For the Children****, the story of my family's escape from Stalinist Hungary during the 1956 revolution when I was seven years old. Chapters 13 to 16 relate how, after several unsuccessful attempts to get across the border to Austria, my parents' dreams were finally realized when, just after St. Nicholas Day, the start of the Christmas season in Europe, we succeeded. It recaps the story of our first few days of freedom, and the warm reception by the Austrians, including relatives, and then – as if the trauma of the escape were not enough – of the difficulties we encountered to get to our destination, Canada. It tells of our arrival with nothing to our new homeland and of the wonderful welcome we received from Canadians. These are times I shall never forget, and the vivid memories flood back each Christmas, making the holiday even more special.*

Chapter 13

We — and the small band of refugees — trudged along behind the Austrian border guards for what seemed like an eternity. Finally, from the bottom of a small hill, up which the dirt path snaked, we could see the dark shapes of a small cluster of houses emerge around the silhouette of the steeple. We quickened our pace, and within moments, we were in the outskirts of a tiny village. An Austrian village.

Deutschkreutz[1]. Our — that is, my — first contact with the western world. The Free World.

That first glimpse — the church steeple on top of the small rise — is etched in my memory. As is the date: December seventh, 1956. The date of our escape, of our final and successful attempt to cross the Iron Curtain.

My mind was racing ahead, punchy with lack of sleep and the exhilaration of the moment.

What would life be like, out there, in the great unknown?

Would I be able to learn the language, adapt to the customs, the details required for daily existence in this foreign atmosphere, waiting for me in the darkness up ahead?

Would I make friends?

What would school be like? And what will I become when I grow up? What would have become of me had I stayed in Hungary? The secret police did tell my father that we would never be allowed to go to university.

Thoughts like these paraded through my brain, tripping and tumbling over each other, not staying long enough to await an answer. I knew that my parents, and all the refugees in the little group, must have had similar ideas cross their brains. Of course, for my parents, the questions were much, much weightier than for me: they had three children to think of beside themselves.

The current of events we were floating in, weightless, was too swift, much too fast, to permit even a glimmer of comprehension. We only sensed that our lives were going through a period of momentous change, but we did not, and could not, fathom the extent and direction of that change.

*****

I returned from my reverie to the real world just as small houses started to materialize on either side of the road out of the darkness. I was astonished to note that they did not seem any different from the ones back across the border in the Hungary we had just left behind. They, too, were low huts, covered with what seemed to be colored stucco — some white, some yellow, some blue — and with little fenced in gardens. Only they all seemed to be less run down, in better condition than the ones in war-torn Hungary.

People were sleeping inside, snoring, dreaming, exactly as they were in any village in Hungary. And they would get up just the same way in the morning and go about the daily chores that permitted survival and occupied life. Except that the paraphernalia of existence — those all-important determinants, such as language, such as freedom to do and say as one pleases, the opportunities that make life more palatable, the supply of goods, and many other qualitative aspects of living — were different on one side from those on the other. It was for these very reasons that my parents had decided to leave the 'other', and chosen 'this' — this, of which we had only a vague inkling. The 'other' must have been really intolerable for them to prefer the unknown that lay ahead. But they were young and brave, and willing to build a new life. They would not sink, I was sure of that.

We finally came to the church, with its tall steeple dominating the hamlet and the countryside from its central location right on the main square of Deutschkreutz. With a reflex motion my father had inculcated in me in defiance of Hungary's Communist authorities, I crossed myself as we passed in front of it[2]. As I did, I realized that I no longer had to hide or be ashamed of such overt demonstrations of what I then believed in, or indeed, of who I was.

Right behind the church was the high school. It was here that the two Austrian guards were leading us. They opened a small gate — (oh, how its creak reminded me of the noise made by the gate of our fence in Buda!) — and shepherded us up the flagstone path to the door of the school. Someone opened it from the inside. Light streamed out to meet us, and we were quickly ushered in from the cold and dark into the warm and well-lit corridor of the Austrian school.

We were received by a chubby, middle-aged woman and a bald man in a Tyrolean cardigan, who now took us in hand, while the tired border guards left to make their way home through the quiet streets of Deutschkreutz, to bed and some well-deserved sleep. It was three o'clock in the morning, and they had waited a full six hours for us out there in the cold.

Our new guides led us along the school's hallway to a cozily lit classroom, where mattresses had been strewn all around. A desk had been pulled over to the door, behind which sat a woman with glasses and hair up in a bun, who took our names and other pertinent information, such as where in Hungary we were from, and the names and addresses of relatives or friends living in Austria. All these data were dutifully entered into a diary under December the seventh. As we were being duly "processed", another woman was already handing around mugs of steaming hot tea. We were then finally allowed to drag ourselves over to the lined up bare mattresses, on which we collapsed and gladly stretched out to rest our tired legs.

I barely had enough energy to kick my shoes off and lay down fully clothed. Someone — I think my mother — threw a blanket over me, and I dozed off, lulled into sleep by the drone of the exhausted but excited voices of the newly arrived adults, who were not given their peace until they recounted their adventures to their new hosts and swapped stories with their previously escaped neighbors on the mattresses. After all, many of these people who were welcoming us with such warmth were of Hungarian origin; almost all had someone back there behind the Iron Curtain. For this was Burgenland, the area of transition between the two formerly great and "equal" partners of the Austro-Hungarian monarchy. Prior to the First World War, Burgenland had been a part of Hungary, and only became Austrian in a close vote in a referendum held by the victors since they could not decide where it belonged[3]. This is the land where the Eszterházy princes had their dominions, where Haydn, Liszt and Lchár came from. These were our brothers receiving us, and it was all so familiar, reminding us of home. Which made us all the more grateful.

*****

When I woke, in the early morning, my eyes at first had trouble getting used to the bright light streaming in through the large windows of the classroom. At home in Buda, there were curtains on the windows of the room Peter, Clara and I shared — I was used to sleeping in darkness — so I knew immediately that something was not right. As I started to look around, my bewildered fear grew to alarming proportions: where was I, who were these sleeping bodies strewn around on bare mattresses all over the classroom? The shock, though, slowly began to set the wheels of my power of reasoning back into motion, and I soon remembered the epic events of the night before, of the last few days. All that, however, seemed like a dream my mind had conjured up, and the only proof that it had been for real, was the fact that I was not in my bed in Budapest, but on a mattress in a classroom in some village in Austria. My eyes roamed around the room and finally fixed on my parents, over in a corner warming their hands on steaming mugs of coffee — a reassuring picture that helped my fear and anxiety ebb away.

When she saw that I was stirring, my mother came over to my mattress and handed her cup to me. I gladly took it and relished the warmth: this, too, was proof that we were living abnormal times, for at home in Budapest, I would not be allowed to drink coffee.

"Hurry and wash up, and then you can come with us to the post office to call Gida bácsi[4] in Vienna."

Nine years earlier, Peter's birth had not stopped Gida bácsi from going to the soccer game between Austria and Hungary in Vienna alone, without my parents[5]. As he recounted to us later, it was not until the Hungarian spectators were getting back on board the boat that would take them down the Danube to Budapest that Gida bácsi saw his chance. While the other passengers were boarding, Gida bácsi quietly lowered himself down into the water on the other side of the boat and swam across the river. Once on shore, he eventually made his way to the American zone. Since then, he had done well, setting up a refrigeration business, and my parents were sure that he would be eagerly awaiting news of our escape. We knew that he would help us.

When, after performing my cursory morning ablutions, I skipped back into the big classroom where we had spent the night, I saw that my father was obtaining instructions on how to get to the post office, as well as some change from one of the kindly Austrians to make the telephone call. I was curious and keen to explore the new world lying out there beyond the fence that — as I remembered from the night before — surrounded the school. So, Peter, Clara and I eagerly followed our parents, navigating our way among the archipelago of mattresses and then out the front door into the sunny but cold new day.

We wandered into the main square. Life was just barely starting to get underway in this sleepy little Austrian village. My eyes followed my father's glance up the church steeple, where I noticed that the clock read only ten minutes before eight.

The post office did not open until eight, so my father suggested that we wander around the village. That is what we did, whiling away the time window-shopping in the small square at ten to eight on our first morning of freedom. Perhaps sacrilegious — or was it that we were prematurely succumbing to the decadent bourgeois materialism that was supposed to permeate the West?

First, a closed bank. Nothing to see there. But we were at least reassured by this symbol of wealth: we would not suffer poverty in the capitalist Free World.

Next to the bank, a pharmacy with shutters still down. The most exciting thing in this window was a beautifully calligraphed sign giving the time of opening as ten o'clock.

Then the window of a ladies' clothing shop. Here, my mother stopped when she saw the display.

"Oh, look at those dresses! What a beautiful cut! And look at that material, Péter. It must cost a fortune!" she burst out, unable to contain her enthusiasm.

It did not take much to excite the fancy of newly arrived refugees from behind the Iron Curtain: even the quality and variety available in a small Austrian border village surpassed the selection offered in Budapest, renowned then in Eastern Europe as the "Paris of the East" for its shopping possibilities.

While we were standing there in front of the ladies' wear shop — my mother gawking at the beautiful dresses and suits, wondering if she would ever be able to own even one of those fashionable articles of clothing — we became aware of the wafting of a tantalizing aroma: the smell of bread freshly drawn from the oven. Our attention followed our noses to the next shop, which, as we had surmised from the delicious smell, proved to be a bakery. We gazed hungrily through the door at the golden loaves of bread being taken out, one by one, from the old-fashioned brick oven, and carefully placed on the counter to cool. My father jingled the Austrian coins in his pocket, perhaps hoping that after his call, there might still be enough for just one such fresh loaf that we could tear apart, like tigers, with our hands and teeth.

After the bakery, came a furniture store. My parents stopped and lingered wistfully for a moment, but Peter and I did not find the chairs and tables and armoire in the window all that interesting. We ran ahead to the next shop: a toy store! The window was brimming with an array of amazing things: luxurious cars and dolls and wooden trains and box games and airplane models. Relics of Saint Nicholas' Day — the boot overflowing with candies, nuts, and dried fruits — although Peter and I knew that we had done a lot better this year, for we had been given, as a present from Old Saint Nick, our freedom. The devil, too, was there in the window, lurking in one corner, looking mean and ugly — and this time vanquished — with a switch made of branches in his claws, and coals under his hooves, which was all that you got if you were bad. Farther toward the back of the store, we could even see a Christmas tree, all decorated with candies and ornaments. We were enthusiastically pointing out these reminders of the Christmas spirit to each other with "oohs" and "aahs" when my parents finally caught up with us and brought us back to earth.

"Come on, children! It's already ten past eight," my father said, beckoning in the direction of the post office. "Let's go call Gida bácsi. I would like to catch him before he leaves for work."

*****

We found the post office, just around the corner from the toyshop. My father gave Gida bácsi's number to the man behind the counter to place the call, and anxiously went into the second booth along the wall. After a tense pause, there was a loud ring, and through the paper-thin walls we could hear my father's excited voice greet his cousin. A few moments later, my father emerged from the booth, beaming.

"Gida is going to Steyr for the day on business, but he promised to send his assistant, Oskar, in his car to fetch us. We're supposed to meet

Oskar at noon in front of some inn — the Gasthof Wienerblut," he reported with satisfaction. "We'll be in Vienna before Gida returns. He told me that he has been waiting for this call ever since the Revolution broke out in October. Well, we'll see him this evening for sure."

We were not at all eager to go back to the depressing refugee camp after this wonderful news. So, we strolled, at a leisurely pace, around Deutschkreutz, playing tourist in this little border village. We even relinquished the sunlight for a moment, for the cool darkness of the church on the square, in order to give silent thanks for our newfound freedom.

When we finally returned to the camp, the citizens of Deutschkreutz were just handing around breakfast trays with delicious Viennese coffee — *mit Schlag*[6] — and those Kaiser rolls we had seen in the bakery, with fresh butter and homemade jams. Our hunger, therefore, did not go unsatisfied.

At quarter to twelve, we wandered over toward the Gasthof Wienerblut. Sure enough, Oszi arrived in Gida bácsi's little red Fiat shortly after twelve, and with much backslapping and cheek kissing, officially welcomed us to Austria.

Together we walked back to the camp, where Oszi signed some papers to attest to the fact that he would assume responsibility for us on this journey to Vienna, and that once in the capital, he personally would make sure that we would obtain all the requisite papers to stay in Austria.

We said goodbye to the camp — to our kind hosts and the other refugees. We were the lucky ones, as we only had to spend one night in the lager. Many unfortunate refugees from the East ended up staying for weeks and months, some even for years in the most miserable conditions imaginable in such camps, waiting for some country or other to accept them. This, no doubt, was for them an unfavorable introduction to the western world — however, infinitely preferable to the prospect of going back or staying behind the Iron Curtain. Yes, we were lucky; we had been vouched for by acquaintances in Austria almost immediately.

After a filling and tasty meal of *Wienerschnitzel, Rösti* [7]and cucumber salad at the Gasthof Wienerblut, we set off in Gida bácsi's car for Vienna. The car was only a small Fiat — not a Mercedes, not an American car — but for someone from Eastern Europe, the ride was a luxurious experience indeed — even though I was crammed in the back seat between Peter on one side and my mother with Clara in her lap on the other. Red and shiny on the outside, with tan leather upholstery on the inside, it was a beautiful sight to behold. How smoothly its engine purred along, and how well it took the curves along the hilly Austrian highways! Oszi bácsi — for by this time we were calling him by his nickname too, incongruously though, with the deferential "bácsi", or "uncle", suffixed thereto — drove like a maniac. But for me in the back seat, this was the thrill of my life. Much, much better than the roller coaster ride in the Vidám Park, the amusement park in Pest, where on festive occasions my grandparents used to take us.

Despite the initial exhilaration, I must have fallen into a deep sleep. For the next thing I remember is waking to the stopping and starting of the car in city traffic. We were in a big metropolis, with thousands of bright neon lights just being turned on all over. Bleary eyed, I asked my mother where we were.

"Vienna," she answered, beaming.

I gazed out the window of the Fiat: a clock on some official looking building read quarter after five. I remember asking my parents what an enormous, blinking red neon sign that spelled "C-o-c-a C-o-l-a" stood for. They didn't know either, and my father asked Oszi bácsi, in German. A few seconds later, after a hearty laugh from our chauffeur and an involved explanation, the only word of which I understood was "American", I got my delayed answer.

"It's a sweet American drink for children."

This was our real welcome to the West.

Chapter 14

Vienna. Wien. City of the waltz, of dreams divine. The former capital of the Austro-Hungarian Empire. Gateway to the East — but for us, refugees from behind the Iron Curtain, it proved to be the portal to the West. And to freedom. Finally, after nine long years of waiting — for, by all rights, my parents should have been here in 1947, and I should have been born at least an Austrian, if not a Canadian — we found ourselves in the former Imperial capital.

My parents hoped though, that it would be only for a short while. Vienna was only meant to be a steppingstone on our way to Canada.

But what a steppingstone! We had never experienced such luxury, such abundance, such extravagance. Our Austrian relatives — some of whom had married into our family still during the time of the monarchy, while others, like Gida, had managed to get out and make a life for themselves there after the Second World War and the Communist takeover in Hungary — were so kind, and treated us so well, that we knew we would never be able to repay their hospitality.

For example, when we arrived in Vienna, Oszi bácsi took us straight around the Ring — the broad avenue that circles downtown Vienna — to Kärtnerstrasse[8] and the exquisitely reconstructed Staatsoper[9], which had only been open for a little over a year since its reconstruction — where he pulled up in front of an expensive looking hotel.

The Bristol. Gida bácsi had reserved a two-room suite for us here, since he was afraid there would not be ample room in his modest apartment to house this big family of five properly. And, as Oszi said when my father started to protest, Gida bácsi did not want us to feel like poor Eastern European refugees. He wanted us to feel that we were citizens of the Western World. That was no doubt partly why he had chosen the Bristol: it had been the seat of the American High Command after the War.

We thanked Oszi bácsi for having come and picked us up in Deutschreutz, and he was off again, this time to meet Gida bácsi at the train station. As soon as he left, we started settling into our new home — simply another in a series of temporary residences, which, however, were getting to be more and more luxurious — washed up and stretched out on our beds. It had already been a long day after a long night.

*****

My father could not wait to announce to our relatives and friends in Vienna that we were there. His first call was to Alfréd bácsi[10]. This distinguished gentleman, whose daughters had summered at Akarattya[11] and were friends of my father's older sister, Klára, had been the last Chief of Staff of the Austrian armed forces prior to the Anschluss with Germany, retiring in disgust at the enthusiasm shown by many of his countrymen for Hitler and Nazism. To this day, there is a plaque at the entrance to the building where he lived to commemorate the valiant but unused military plans he had drawn up to defend Vienna against Nazi Germany.

Alfréd bácsi had a booming voice, so that we could not help but hear his end of the conversation as well. "Thank God, you're finally here, Péter. We have been waiting for you since the first shots were fired in Budapest. I have been holding the guest room in readiness for you. Your beds are made; Herta has even laid out the towels for you. Come right over." Old Alfréd bácsi greeted my father as if he were one of his very own nephews.

It took my father some time to convince Alfréd bácsi that we already had a roof over our heads for the night, and that, for the moment, it would be easier for us to stay put in the hotel where we had installed ourselves.

"Well then, come tomorrow. Gida should not have to pay for those rooms when I have enough space in my apartment to house an entire Division of the Austrian army. Besides, I am sure that you will agree that it is much more pleasant to stay with me than in a hotel."

"Yes, Onkel Alfred. Of course. And thank you. We will come tomorrow then. What time would be convenient for you?"

"Come as soon as you can. I — Herta and Judith as well — am dying to see you. Come in the morning already — any time after seven o'clock — I am an early riser. We could have breakfast together." Alfréd bácsi could not hide his eagerness to inspect his "relatives" from the East.

"To tell you the truth, Onkel Alfred, in the morning I would like to go to the police station to get our refugee papers — the *Flüchtlingsscheine*, isn't that what they are called? And then, if time permits, to the Canadian Embassy to apply for a visa."

"The Canadian Embassy! What in the devil's name for? You're not going to go to that far-off, uncivilized land, not while I am still alive! You must be joking! Tell me you are not serious! Come over as soon as you can, Péter. So that I can talk some sense into your head!"

"Well, I would like to get the paperwork started. And of course, the more options we have, the better."

"But good Lord, Péter, don't you know tomorrow is a holiday? Nothing is open, certainly not any police station, nor the Canadian Embassy!"

"I would just like to try, on the off chance ..."

"All right, Péter. Run around in the morning, if you must." Alfréd bácsi was losing his patience with his stubborn refugee "relative". "Why don't you come for lunch, then? Herta will make Tafelspitz[12], which I remember was not just Franz-Josef's, but also your favorite. At one, shall we say?"

*****

A few minutes after my father hung up, the telephone rang. Gida bácsi was downstairs in the lobby, calling on one of the house phones. He was coming up.

My father paced around: a knock, and then he opened the door. For a moment, the two cousins looked each other in the eyes and then embraced like only East European males embrace. When the bodies disentangled, I saw that this Gida bácsi, of whom I had heard so much, was about the same age as my father and just as blond. Perhaps a little stouter, and shorter. The family resemblance was obvious — after, all Gida bácsi was my father's first cousin.

"How long has it been, Péter, since we have seen each other?" The voice was deeper, fuller.

"More than nine years, nine long years!" My father looked at Gida bácsi as if he were looking into the past, trying to recapture its flow.

"And Lilyke, you look as lovely as ever!" Gida bácsi paid tribute to my mother's celebrated beauty. He used the Hungarian diminutive suffix "-ke", for when he left Budapest, my mother was still a teenager. Nineteen years old.

"The children, too, are beautiful, just as I imagined them to be." Gida bácsi turned his attention to Peter and me, still sitting shyly on one of the beds. "No one can say they don't have handsome parents. But I must admit, they do look hungry," here he winked at us, "and in that, too, there is a family resemblance. Péter, I know you are always ready to eat, and I haven't had any supper yet either, so why don't we go somewhere really nice for a bite to eat. And to celebrate. Over dinner, you can tell me all about your escape. And the Revolution. I am dying to hear a firsthand account."

In my eagerness to go and have a good meal, I jumped up from the head of the bed where I had been slouching, one elbow poised on the night table, enjoying every minute of the exchange between my father and this newly rediscovered cousin. As I did so, I knocked over the thermos my mother had left standing on the table next to the lamp. I cringed as I heard the glass inside explode.

Perhaps it was the tension of the last forty-eight hours, or the nagging fear of the unknown that still lay ahead, or the fact that the thermos was our only material possession apart from the clothes we were wearing, or that it had held the life-giving coffee during our several escape attempts. Whatever the reason, my father yelled at me angrily.

"Now see what you've done! Can't you sit still for a moment?"

The noise, the tension, overwhelmed my mother too. Her composure shattered. She broke into tears but was immediately ashamed in front of Gida bácsi. The entire scene was not a good introduction to this relative, whom, I at least, did not know at all, and whom my parents had not seen for almost ten years. My clumsy act seemed to crystallize the distance between the inept, poor East and the smooth, sophisticated West.

But finally, it was Gida bácsi who eased us away from the potential abyss of complete emotional disintegration.

"Péter, it's all right. Don't worry." Gida bácsi touched my father's elbow with his right hand, while with his left, he reached inside his pocket for his billfold and handed my father what looked like a huge wad of folded Austrian money. "Here, I want you to take this. Tomorrow, you can buy yourselves a hundred thermoses and whatever else you need."

"Don't be ridiculous, Gida ..." My father pushed Gida bácsi's outstretched hand and the schillings away.

"But I insist," Gida bácsi cut him short. "You must take this money, if for no other reason, then for my sake ..."

"Gida, no ..."

"... Here. When I first arrived in Vienna after the War, an old Hungarian peasant, who didn't know me at all, gave me some money, just like this, to help me start a new life. I protested, but he insisted to the point of embarrassment that I take it. And when I vowed to him that I would repay him someday, he said no, I was not to repay him, but to give the money to some needy Hungarian in the future. So, this is my chance to settle my debt with the old man. Plus, you are a relative and a friend, so I may even be cheating a little. In any case, I insist that you take the money; sometime in the future, you too can help a Hungarian who is down and out. Or any refugee in need of a leg up."

My father muttered a shy "thank you" as he carefully folded the money and put it in his pocket. "And I will pay you back ..."

"But now let's go and eat!" Gida bácsi returned to that all-important topic I had so unfortunately interrupted.

Our generous uncle instructed the taxi to take us to the Hotel Sacher. Walking through the portals of this celebrated Viennese institution, I could not suppress the "oohs" and "aahs" of callow amazement. My incredulity was only exceeded by my reverence, when, as we entered the elegant dining room, Gida bácsi explained to us that this was where the famous Sachertorte we all loved so much had been invented, and that the best chocolate cake in the world was still baked here. Everything else that went under the name was a mere imitation.

My reverence, that is, and my appetite. Both Peter and I just ate and ate, as if this was our last supper — and not just the very first one in the West. A delicious mushroom soup — my favorite — followed by pheasant, and of course, for dessert, Sachertorte. My poor parents, however, could hardly get a mouthful in edgewise; they were so busy recounting the life-or-death adventures we had just experienced. Strange, already how far away it all seemed, as we sat there in the plush velvet seats, gorging ourselves on Sachertorte. Another life, perhaps.

But it was sure not hard to get used to this one!

*****

The next morning, my parents rose early. When Peter and I stirred in the adjoining smaller room, my father came over to Peter's bed and gave him instructions for the day. We were to be ready to go to Alfréd bácsi's by twelve noon.

Deep down, my father could not have been too optimistic about being able to obtain the "Flüchtlingsscheine" or refugee papers — let alone succeed in seeing someone at the Canadian Embassy. As Alfréd bácsi had reminded him, December eighth was not only a Saturday, but also the day of the Immaculate Conception, a holiday in Catholic Austria. However, his perseverance did pay off: the police station was open, not least because of the extraordinary demands being put on officials by the steady flow of refugees from across the Iron Curtain.

In fact, when my parents arrived at the station — at seven o'clock — there were twenty-three immigrants already waiting in line. The Austrian police took their time over each individual they processed, and it was not until eleven-twenty that my parents had in their hands the requisite papers that would allow our family to stay in Austria.

From the police station, my father sent my mother back to the hotel. They were starting to get worried about what we might be up to. Although they had left Peter in charge, they were skeptical of the capacity of such an arrangement to last for an extended period of time. Too often in the past, the result had been black eyes, torn shirts, or broken vases.

"I think I will still go and see what I can achieve at the Canadian Embassy. Even though according to Alfréd bácsi, they are supposed to be closed as well. Who knows, we might get lucky there, too."

Chapter 15

As my father later recounted over lunch, when he arrived at the Canadian Embassy, its shuttered windows gave it the look of an impenetrable fortress. On the massive, carved wooden doors a sign read “Closed” in German and in English. However, he rang the bell again and again until someone finally came and opened the door a crack.

He was somewhat taken aback by the man’s casual dress — wrinkled corduroy pants and faded plaid shirt — and quickly concluded that this man could not be the duty clerk but had to be part of the cleaning crew. Nevertheless, he realized he was not in a position to be choosy.

“I am very sorry to bother you, sir,” he addressed the dubious looking employee of the Embassy as politely as he could, “but I would like to emigrate to Canada with my family. We have just escaped from Hungary. My mother, brother and sister[13] are already Canadian residents. Here are our Flüchtlingsscheine.” And he proudly produced the papers he had acquired just moments before at the police station.

“I’m sorry. I can’t help you,” the man dressed like a janitor answered. “You’ll have to come back tomorrow.”

“Could you the please be kind enough to tell me, sir, what I have to do to get a visa for Canada?” My father persisted, hoping to get whatever advantage he could by gleaning the slightest bit of information from this employee of the Canadian Embassy.

“Well, you have to fill out an application form. And get it stamped for an interview with the Consul. After your interview, you have to pass a medical examination. But come back tomorrow and talk to the guys from Immigration. They’ll be able to help you. I’m just the weekend Security Officer.”

"Would it be possible to get one of those application forms?" My father quickly blurted out before the official could close the door. "I would like to study it, to make sure that I will not make a mistake in filling it out. I would really be grateful if you would be so kind as to give me one."

The Security Officer — my father was still not completely convinced that he was not the janitor — was, by this time, getting quite fed up with the polite, but inquisitive foreigner. If not out of kindness or compassion, then just to get rid of him, the official stepped back into some office and came out with one of those precious forms.

My father — smelling success — decided to try the man's patience just a little longer.

"And would it be possible to get the form stamped now for an interview?"

"I'm sorry. I've already done more for you than I'm authorized to." The bureaucrat in the man came to the fore. "Come back early tomorrow. You can get the form stamped then." The Security Officer was ready to close the door.

"What time does the lineup usually start?" My father tried for one last bit of information.

"Oh, it's hard to say, but I'd get here pretty early, if I were you," the official said elusively. "People are usually waiting already when the doors open at eight-thirty."

My father thanked the man profusely and fled with his treasure. He was convinced that his scouting trip to the Embassy had been worthwhile. Whoever that man in the sloppy clothes was — Security Officer, bureaucrat, or janitor — to my father he would always be an angel in disguise.

*****

Alfréd bácsi lived in a large apartment, in a building owned by the Austrian Ministry of Defense and rented out to senior officers and pensioners at highly subsidized rates. His was one of the nicest: a bright, corner apartment on the fifth floor overlooking the Urania[14] and the Ring. He and his two daughters, Herta and Judit — still, in later life, known endearingly in the family as "the Jansa girls", since they never married — occupied eight rooms with high ceilings, linked by French doors. A maid and a butler had separate chambers at the top of the building. There were mirrors all over, like in a ballroom. In fact, the French doors between the dining and drawing rooms could be opened to make just that: a large salle with parquet floors for dancing. Art treasures hung on the walls and luxurious Persian carpets softened the tread underfoot.

Over lunch, my father could not keep the secret for very long that he had obtained the "Flüchtlingsscheine" that morning, and that he had also managed to get an application form for an entry visa to Canada. When Alfréd bácsi heard mention made of Canada again, he lit into a tirade.

"Oh, yes. I knew there was something important that I wanted to talk to you about. Canada. Why on earth would you want to go to Canada, of all places? It is so far away, and so cold; people freeze to death there. That country is still a wild frontier land, with no culture to speak of. It is not a good place to bring up your children. Why, you could have such a wonderful life here! Gida could give you a job — he has that refrigerator factory, doesn't he? And you could live here, at my place, until you earn enough to set up on your own. Besides, here, you would be close to your homeland, and in a few years, I am sure the political situation will have eased so that you will be able to visit Lily's parents regularly. Or they can come here — it's just a few hours away. They are not getting any younger either and the time will soon come when they will not be able to undertake a journey longer than a couple of hours."

"Dear Onkel Alfred," my father started into the firm argument he had prepared against the objections he expected from Alfréd bácsi on his way back from the Canadian Embassy. "We have gone through this on our own with Lily a number of times. We considered staying in Austria for some of those very reasons you have mentioned. But, in the end, they are not enough to keep us here. As you know, most of my family is already in Canada. Although I have never actually visited, and I cannot honestly claim to know it yet, in some ways I feel that Canada is already my new homeland. But what is most appealing to us, is that it is a free and peaceful country. Here in Austria, the Soviets would still be breathing down our necks. They just left last year. At any moment, another war could break out. I am tired of war. I am tired of always having to accommodatc myself to different régimes. I want to be left alone to raise my children decently and honestly. And all indications so far suggest that I would be able to do that best in Canada. That is why we are going there, if we can. I am willing to put up with a little physical discomfort — such as the cold — and some emotional distress — such as being far away from some relatives. Sometimes, one has to make choices."

"Yes, we decided already back in Budapest that we would try to go to Canada." My mother lent her support to my father. "And only if that didn't succeed, would we consider staying here ..." She hesitated, knowing that what she was about to say would deflate Alfréd bácsi. "... But in fact, Austria would probably be our fourth or fifth choice, after the United States and England. Maybe Australia. Somehow, it is just too close to all the misery, all the injustice that we are trying to leave behind."

This combined and well-reasoned resistance on the part of my parents silenced poor old Alfréd bácsi. He went off to his bedroom for his siesta, muttering something into his jowls and instructing Herta and Judit to look after us.

*****

We, too, spent a good part of the afternoon resting. My parents especially were in need of a nap, since they had spent the entire morning rushing around to get the papers for us. Plus, no doubt they were exhausted from all the tension and effort of the last couple of days.

After a few hours of sleep, we got up to look around the famously beautiful Imperial capital. We allowed ourselves the luxury of playing tourist. In fact, what a wonderful way to see Vienna that was! All expenses paid, through the generosity of kind-hearted relatives, and without a worry in the world! That is, if my parents could forget the 'minor' worries of finding a new homeland, of how we would get there, of building a future for themselves and their children.

But that afternoon, we did just that: we forgot where we had come from, where we were trying to go, and all the obstacles we had surmounted so far and those we still had to cross.

At the sight of the extravagant supply of goods in the shop windows in Vienna — there were only a few days left until Christmas — my parents' resolve to spend as little of the money Gida bácsi had given them as possible, broke down. They bought all sorts of 'bare necessities' that, to us, could not help but seem luxuries: shirts, underwear, gloves to replace the ones knit by Mama[15] that I had left in the Gasthof Wienerblut in Deutschkreutz. There were moments during that afternoon stroll when my father could not resist the temptation of splurging — for example, when we came across a vendor on Kärtnerstrasse selling Dinky toys, American made toy cars — and our pleading eyes told him that this was what Peter and I had been dreaming of for years. Or just some piping-hot chestnuts from a little man near the Hofburg[16], stoking a fire in a blackened brazier. Or some Viennese coffee — *mit Schlag* — and Apfelstrudel at the Café Central, full of dignified Viennese dowagers and intellectuals, with the life-sized full portraits of Franz Josef and the Empress Sissi staring out at us from the back wall.

Nor could my parents quell their curiosity to try Coca Cola — even though Oszi bácsi had told them that it was a sweet children's drink.

But of course, this became a more expensive venture than they had anticipated, because all of us clamored for a sip, and the one little bottle they first bought was not enough for five.

My father almost spat it out.

"My God, this is terrible. I swear I will never have another sip of this as long as I live! I don't see how people can prefer this to beer or wine. Or just plain water." (He kept his promise, as far as I know.)

"Now, Géza. Don't drink too much!" my mother exhorted. "It's addictive. It's made from cocaine, a drug that is very bad for you. It makes you go crazy…"

So, in the end, a lot of Gida bácsi's money was spent on non-essential things, out of curiosity and self-indulgence. But it was Christmastime, and during the last few months, we had gone through so many hardships, so many disappointments, that we deserved the opportunity to let ourselves go a little. And it was fun, really fun — as we found out — to spend money!

I only hope that Gida bácsi eventually forgave my parents for yielding to these little acts of temptation with his — or was it the old peasant's? — money.

*****

At six o'clock the next morning, my father made his way over again to the Canadian Embassy. By the time he got there, a boisterous crowd of Hungarians had already formed what resembled a queue to wait for the Immigration Office to open. From six-twenty until eight-thirty, my father, and an ever-growing number of refugees, shifted from one foot to the other, rubbed hands together in the cold of the Austrian winter morning, and cursed the slow bureaucracy of the Embassy.

Several minutes after eight-thirty, however, a small, nervous clerk came out through the large wooden doors with a beige file under his arm, whistling nonchalantly, and strolled along the line, around the corner, where instinct or experience told him he would find the end of the queue. My father, having become acquainted the day before with the casualness of Embassy personnel, gambled on the significance of this clerk's sudden appearance after two and a half hours of patient waiting. Out of the corner of one eye he ascertained that nothing was happening at the door of the Embassy, and quickly followed the clerk around the corner. He managed to catch up to the official, just as he was handing out the last of the application forms to the lucky refugees who happened to be near the end of the line.

My father looked over the shoulder of one of the fortunate recipients to learn to his jubilation that this was the same form he had received from the Security Officer the day before. Exactly the same, that is, except for the fact that the form in front of his eyes was stamped with the official seal of the Embassy of Canada, underneath which, handwritten in ink, was a certain hour of the day. The form neatly folded in the inside breast pocket of his jacket, however, had no such seal and no time written on it.

"All those with forms, follow me," the clerk gave instructions. "There is a bus around the corner to take you to an interview with the Consul, in whose presence you will appear at the time stated on the forms you have just received. You are to fill these forms out and hand them to an official before you enter your interview. Afterwards, you will proceed directly to your interview in the same building. Good luck."

The taciturn man turned on his heels with no apparent comprehension of, or remorse for, the gross injustice he had committed in the interest of expediency. It did not seem to matter to him that people had been waiting for hours — some all night — at the head of the line. It was so much easier to hand the forms out around the corner where the bus was waiting with engine purring and leave those up front ignorant of what was happening. Only so many refugees could be processed — did it matter to Canada whether those who lined up in the cold darkness of dawn, or those who arrived at the Embassy a few moments before it opened, got first crack at immigrating to Canada?

My father, adopting a loose interpretation of the clerk's words — followed the official and the fifty or so lucky people who had received the legitimate form, to where the bus was waiting. He stayed back, however, and cunningly observed what the procedure was to get on the bus. When he saw that the others were allowed on simply by waving their forms, he pulled the unstamped piece of paper the Security Guard had given him the day before from his pocket and boarded with no trouble.

The bus pulled away from the curb with a lurch and careened at high speed through the streets of Vienna. He looked around at the other passengers with a lump of guilt forming in his throat. They were all holding in their hands application forms that had been franked, whereas the piece of paper he had inconspicuously replaced in his breast pocket did not have the official insignia of the Canadian Embassy stamped on it.

It was only then that he noticed that sitting right in front of him were two ladies and a small boy, all three holding and reading the necessary forms. The official stamps and the written in times simply glared up at my father. As calmly and as politely as he could, he addressed the woman directly in front of him, who appeared to be the mother of the child, and the self-appointed leader of the small group.

"Excuse me, Madam, but I am wondering if you would be so kind as to consider giving me one of your forms. The three of you only need two: one for your friend and one for yourself. Minors are entitled to enter Canada on their parents' form." The night before, my father had studied the fine print on the form the Security Officer had given him.

"No, I am sorry. We stood in line for these forms, and we are not going to give them to anybody. We may need all of them," the woman answered with a cold look.

"You know, Madam, you would be helping five people, not just one. Back in Vienna, I have a wife and three little children whose fates depend on whether I can get another such form." He whipped out a family portrait from his wallet. "Here they are, the darlings. And you really do not need the extra form. It says right on the back page — if you would turn it over — there toward the bottom, that children under twenty-one years of age don't need to apply separately for a visa."

The lady was duly impressed by my father's thorough knowledge of Canadian immigration regulations — if not by the picture of his family — but she was still not prepared to yield the valuable form.

"You know, Madam, if you don't believe me, when we get to wherever this bus is supposed to take us, why don't you and I go together to one of the officials — the Consul himself if you please — and ask them whether your son needs a separate form to apply to get into Canada. If he does, I promise I'll stop bothering you, and I apologize ahead of time for having been a nuisance. But if he doesn't, then you can safely give the extra form to me and help a family of five — rather than throw away this opportunity for a Hungarian family to go to Canada by giving the unused form back to the Immigration officials. I, my wife, and my children, would be eternally grateful to you."

"My dear Nelly, what the man says is entirely logical," the other woman — her sister or whoever it was — piped up. "We simply cannot lose if we follow the procedure he proposes. And we might end up being able to help another family, who like we, are trying to get to Canada. Why don't we agree?"

The older woman's words provided the extra push the woman with the child needed, for she finally agreed to go to the Consul or whoever with my father as soon as the bus arrived at its destination.

*****

After another ten minutes or so, the bus pulled to a halt outside what appeared to be a *Bierstube* somewhere on the outskirts of Vienna.

My father stayed right behind the woman as she got off the bus and grabbed the child's free hand. He dragged the child and the two women straight to the official looking gentleman sitting behind a large desk just inside the remodeled former drinking establishment.

"Excuse me, sir, but could you please inform us whether children need to make a visa application separately from their parents to enter Canada?"

"No, sir, only one application per adult — that is, anyone over twenty-one years of age — is required. Minors can enter on either parent's visa."

My father turned to the woman with the child, hoping that the official's response had settled the matter once and for all, but before he could say anything, the lady, wanting to eliminate the lingering doubt still in her mind, rephrased the man's answer in her own words.

"You mean to say, that my sister, my child and I only need two forms for all three of us to be able to get into Canada?"

"That is entirely correct, Madam," came the reply my father was praying to hear, "that is, as long as you pass the medical examinations."

She and my father thanked the helpful official and then walked to where the sister was waiting with the child.

"Here, why don't you take my form," the woman said, turning to my father, "it has the latest time marked on it. I will use my son's. I still don't know how you will get your wife into Canada as well, since you seem to need one form per adult, but that is your problem, my good sir. Anyway, good luck to you."

My father did not give away the plan that was beginning to formulate in his mind. He rushed back to the official and asked if he could use the telephone on the desk. He called Alfréd bácsi, and instructed him to send my mother and us, the children, to the beer hall where he was, as quickly as possible.

After this important telephone call, he filled out the two forms — the stamped one and the unstamped one — for himself and my mother, put them nervously back in his jacket pocket, and sidled over to where the other refugees were waiting their turn to be interviewed by the Consul.

Fortunately, the time on the franked form was a good couple of hours away, but my father could not help pacing up and down in the reception area. We finally arrived and my father hastily recounted to my mother all that had happened that morning. Only then did he approach the official's table again, this time with us in tow. He pulled the two forms out from his pocket — the one with the stamp and the time on top, the one without, on the bottom — and handed them to the man.

"These are the forms for my wife and myself. Our children are marked on my form."

The official looked up from his perusal of the other refugees' forms, and muttered something under his breath that resembled a "thank you". As he attempted to place my parents' forms in the right time slot in the pile, he glanced at my mother's form, and noticed with a frown that the stamp and the time were missing.

"Hmmm. How odd. They must have forgotten to stamp this form," he grumbled at the irregularity, more to himself than for our benefit, and from the right-hand drawer of his desk, produced the Embassy stamp, with which he franked the form, as he continued, "Happened before … Your wife will have her interview at the same time as you — at eleven AM." The clerk looked at my father, and then proceeded to write the time on my mother's form in clearly legible numbers.

My father's sense of relief was tangible, even for someone only seven years old.

*****

Our turn to see the Consul eventually came. With butterflies in our stomachs, we entered the back room. The Consul told us to sit down, routinely checked through the forms, and asked my father a few questions about his background and intentions. He ended the friendly interrogation by requesting that my father sum up his reasons for wanting to go to Canada.

The Consul was impressed with my father's words. "You'll make good Canadians I am sure of that. But before we can admit you to Canada, you'll have to go through a medical examination. Dr. Brenner will look after you in the next room. Good luck to you and your family. God be with you."

The Consul franked the forms with another stamp and wrote some comments at the bottom with his gold fountain pen. He then handed the forms back to my father, who said "thank you", and we quietly filed out of the room. We only hoped that what the diplomat had written on the form did not differ too much from what he had said to us just a moment before.

*****

The medical examination appeared to be thorough, and apart from the fatigue and stress of the last few months, there seemed to be nothing wrong with us. The examining doctor, Dr. Brenner, stamped the forms yet again, wrote something on them and then told us to take the pieces of paper back to the official at the front desk.

"Well, consider yourselves lucky," the little man at the table in front said after he perused the papers. "You have been officially granted a visa to immigrate to Canada. I suggest that you take the train leaving the Westbahnhof[17] at eight-forty AM on the fifteenth for Genoa to catch the boat departing from there for Halifax in Canada on the morning of the sixteenth. Here are your papers, and good luck to you."

I could see tears in my mother's eyes, tears of happiness. My father, too, could hardly control himself as he prevailed upon the official once again to use his telephone to call Alfréd bácsi to tell him the good news.

It was only after the excitement of being "processed" through this major step in our lives was over that my parents finally paid attention to us. It was then that they noticed that despite successfully passing the medical examination just moments before, Clara did not look well. The anxiety of the last few hours — which even she could not help feeling — must have been too much for her. She was becoming dangerously dehydrated, as she had done on a number of occasions back in Hungary. My parents recognized the symptoms immediately and knew that the situation could develop into something serious: Clara had come close to death several times before from lack of fluids.

Fortunately, we were still only a room away from a doctor, and although it must have occurred to my parents that by taking Clara back to the infirmary, they might be jeopardizing our chances of going to Canada, they did not hesitate for a moment. So, my father went back to the official at the table, and completely disturbed this man's composure by insisting that we be allowed to see Dr. Brenner again. After fifteen minutes or so, we were re-admitted into the examination room, where the doctor took another look at Clara, and gave her some medicine. In answer to my parents' anxious looks, he gave his diagnosis and recommendation.

"Yes, your daughter is definitely sick. Unfortunately, the quick check-up I gave all of you a few moments ago was not designed to catch all such ailments. Under the circumstances, I think it is out of the question that you go on that ship from Genoa, as your form indicates you should. The little girl would not survive the eight-day journey across the Atlantic in a crowded boat on the rough seas. You would do much better to stay here in Vienna until she gains some strength. Or else, try and get on one of those planes provided by the Canadian government to airlift refugees to Canada. It will be difficult because I know they are booked months in advance. But you should inquire at the offices of the International Refugee Organization."

*****

So close, yet still so far. We had escaped, we had all our papers for Canada, but now because Clara was sick, we would have to stay in Vienna indefinitely. Unless, of course, we could get seats on one of those weekly planes that the Canadian government sent to ferry Hungarians with visas to their new homeland. But, as the doctor had said, that was an almost impossible feat.

Nevertheless, the same day still, after lunch with Alfréd bácsi — who did not stop grumbling about his Eastern European relative's relentless pursuit of everything necessary to emigrate to Canada — my father walked over to the Vienna office of the International Refugee Organization, which, as it happened, was in the same "Bezirk", or quarter, as old Jansa's place. The person who greeted him at the reception desk in Hungarian, and with an unusually broad smile on his face, looked familiar, but my father could not quite place him. The man, however, obviously recognized him.

"Please, can you tell me whether keelers can dock here?" the smiling, fit looking man asked my father.

Then my father remembered. The circumstances of their previous meeting immediately flowed back, and a smile appeared on my father's face, too. The summer before, because of my father's good work, our family had been granted the privilege of taking the "22" class sailboat of the state-owned pharmaceutical firm he worked for on a week-long tour around Lake Balaton. The very first night of the holiday, after a long traverse of the lake, we arrived late to the unfamiliar harbor of Keszthely. My father, never having docked there in what for him was a huge boat, yelled out to the only sign of life he could see on the tied-up sailboats.

"Please, can you tell me whether keelers can dock here?"

The answer carried back to him by the wind was a "yes", and the owner of the voice lent a helping hand by catching the rope my father heaved toward the dock and by tying the boat fast. The next night, and just about every night thereafter on this tour, we bumped into this same friendly man and his wife. They seemed to have charted an identical weeklong trip for themselves, with all the same stops on the same dates as us. However, it is difficult to socialize across stretches of water — especially with three children — so my parents never really got to know these friendly people beyond the greeting stage.

Fortunately, though, in spite of the several months and trying times that had elapsed, the two men still recognized each other, and finally introduced themselves.

"We meet again, sailor. It seems that our fates are intertwined. So, you, too, have fled the homeland? Well, congratulations on your success. But what are you doing here? How can I help you?" Székely Gyuri — George Szekely — asked my father.

"I'm trying to get to Canada with my family. And, as at Keszthely, I'm having difficulties coming into port. Perhaps you can help us dock safely once again." My father told the story of how we came to be there — our escape, the visit to the Canadian Consul, the medical examination, Clara's sickness, and the instructions of the doctor.

"Péter, I will see what I can do for you, but I can't promise anything. The first plane is on the nineteenth, and I know for a fact that it is full. There is a waiting list a kilometer long. The next one after that is not until the twenty-eighth; that's full too. There may just be a minute chance that I can get you on that flight, but even that will be next to impossible for all five of you. Maybe Lily and the little one, and you and the boys can take the boat. But don't get your hopes too high. I should let you know something tomorrow."

*****

The next morning, the telephone rang just as we were finishing breakfast at Alfréd bácsi's. It was Székely.

"Péter, the gods must be on your side. It just so happens that this morning, a family of five who were scheduled to go on the flight on the nineteenth, gave up their seats. To make a long story short, Canada was their second choice, and they just found out that they have been granted visas to go to the United States. Believe it or not, there are no families with three children ahead of you on the waiting list. And, since our instructions are to give priority to families with children, I immediately wrote your names in."

"Gyuri, you're a magician. I don't know how I can ever thank you."

"My friend, we sailors have to help each other occasionally. You need to report at Schwechat Airport[18] on the morning of the nineteenth. Come by the office sometime before then, and I will issuc your tickets. See you then."

So, in spite of the momentary setback the recurrence of Clara's illness had caused, we had crossed the last paper hurdle to our entry into Canada. After all the hardships and uncertainties we had endured, we were nearing the end of the odyssey. It seemed that by Christmas, we would finally be in our new homeland.

Chapter 16

Early on the morning of the nineteenth, Alfréd bácsi took us to Schwechat by taxi. We said our goodbyes to this kind "relative" who did not speak a word of Hungarian but had treated us as his own flesh and blood. We would never see him again, for the grand old General died[19] before any of us made it back to Vienna.

We — and many other refugees — were at the airport on the nineteenth as instructed, but the airplane promised by the Canadian government was nowhere to be seen. The noisy group of Hungarians that crowded around the check-in counter was told that due to the worst weather conditions over the North Atlantic in years, the Canadian DC-6 that was supposed to ferry us all to Canada was unable to make it over to Europe. We settled in for an indefinite wait at the airport: we were not allowed to go back into the city, since we had already been cleared for exit through customs and immigration. The Austrian authorities set up a makeshift refugee camp in a warehouse, where we were each assigned a cot to sleep on and issued a couple of blankets to cover us during the cold Central European winter nights.

It is the unrelenting boredom that I remember the most from these days of waiting in that improvised lager. There were no books, no radios, only the odd pack of cards and the standard word games to while the time away. One couldn't really sleep either because someone was always chattering, complaining about this or that, or telling the story of their lives. Or worse still, moaning about the weather.

The airplane did not arrive until the morning of the twenty-third. By the time we were 'processed' one more time, and on the plane, it was well into the afternoon before we were able to leave. We were scarcely able to control our excitement, as first one propeller, then the second one on the same side, and then the two on the other side revved up in turn, and the airplane finally accelerated down the runway and hopped into the air. What a thrill it was for a seven-year-old looking out the window, when the wheels left the ground and we flew into the clouds. But all the more so, since we were on our way to the New World, to a new life! At long last!

*****

On this trip — which for the passengers on board was truly an epic one — the first stop was Le Bourget[20] in Paris. The myriads of lights marking the airport with the red, white and blue hues of the French *tricolore* provided an impressive sight indeed — a rather appropriate one for the Christmas season — as we came out of the clouds and made our final approach to land in the midst of a major downpour. It must have been around eight in the evening when we finally touched down. The pilot's crackling voice informed us over the intercom that there would be an unplanned stopover and we would all have to deplane: the weather over the North Atlantic was still very bad, and we would have to wait in the transit lounge until further notice.

Our hearts sank, and the nervousness returned, but by the time some pretty stewardesses handed out vouchers for dinner — around nine o'clock — our hunger had triumphed. My parents ordered juicy steak frites, while we children ate coq-au-vin, I remember, in the brightly lit restaurant, as we watched several other airplanes take off for exotic places we had never even heard of.

Just after midnight, the announcement came over the loudspeaker that our flight would be leaving soon. We re-boarded the plane at twelve-thirty on the morning of December twenty-fourth. The pilot notified us over the intercom that there had been a change in our flight plans: we would be heading for Santa Maria — one of the Azores Islands — since Iceland, our originally designated refueling stop, was still completely fogged over.

After a long and tedious flight, during which no one got much sleep, and children — including my own sister — were crying or retching all night, we arrived over the lush green Portuguese islands on a beautiful morning just as the sun was rising on the horizon. The plane coasted in over the deep blue sea and touched down on the runway as soon as it was over land. We were told that there would be a stopover of several hours here in Vila do Porto[21], while the machine took on more fuel and provisions for the long trek across the Atlantic to Newfoundland.

So, we disembarked and had a delicious breakfast of strong Brazilian coffee – even I got to taste it – fresh orange juice and croissants, in the airport's pleasant little rooftop restaurant at a table with a clean white tablecloth and a breath-taking view overlooking the ocean. We were served, to our immense surprise and delight, by an old Hungarian émigré with a bald head and a huge moustache. When he overheard us talking in the Magyar language, he broke into tears and cursed the Russians for what they were doing to the homeland of his memories. This waiter, who had left his country during the War, could not resist asking after certain of his relatives, on the off chance that we would know them and be able to give him some news. When we could not help him, the old waiter's incessant questioning turned to the events in Hungary, and my parents tried to satisfy his curiosity as best we could.

After breakfast, we took a walk down a grassy hillside — in glorious sunshine in December, of all things — to the sea, and along a beach studded with pebbles and exotic shells. I felt the water with my fingers: it was much colder than Lake Balaton, or the Danube, the only two major bodies of water I was familiar with. How much bigger, too, the ocean was! As far as you could see, there was water, all around. And presumably, on the other side, toward the west, was Canada.

*****

We took off again, to complete the last leg of our odyssey — the stretch that would finally take us to Canada, the land of our dreams. It proved to be an exhaustingly long haul — ten hours in all — and we passed the time playing cards, reading, making new friends in the cabin or trying to rest.

In fact, my brother Peter, who was curious and continually tried to peek into the cockpit, became so friendly with the pilots, that they allowed him to sit in the co-pilot's seat and pretend that he was driving the plane. Apart from the odd bump — and even when Peter was at the controls — most of the flight seemed to go smoothly. At least I didn't notice anything untoward, for part of the time I was sleeping.

Until the airplane turned its nose into the solid dark grey cloud covering what we had been told would be Newfoundland to attempt a landing, that is. Then we were pitched about, and the many small babies tried to outdo each other wailing in their fear, as some of the passengers resorted to the bags strategically located in the magazine holders on the seat in front of them. It was only after we had landed safely somewhere in the middle of the biggest snowstorm we had ever experienced — Canada, we guessed — and we started to taxi toward a makeshift terminal that the pilot's voice crackled over the intercom to inform us of the flight details.

"Whew. Ladies and gentlemen. We have landed at Gander International Airport, your point of entry into Canada. To be quite honest," the pilot sounded shaken as he continued, "even my co-pilot and I, myself, are saying prayers of thanks at this moment. You will not have realized it, but during the crossing from Santa Maria, the inside propeller on the right-hand side of the plane cracked. Technically, I was supposed to put the bird down on the water — make a crash landing that is — and radio for help. However, given the roughness of the ocean and the many children on board I did not follow the book. Very few if any of us would have survived the cold waters of the stormy North Atlantic. I chose rather to take the risk of going on to Gander with a broken propeller. With hindsight, I am glad to say that it was the right choice. Thank God!"

In spite of this frightening and honest revelation, the mood on the airplane was light and gay as we taxied down the runway toward the little hut that served as control tower, waiting room and customs and immigration building all rolled into one, in this godforsaken outpost of human life. No wonder — this group of refugees had finally arrived in their new homeland, so why should there be no merry-making? And what better timing than Christmas Eve could fate have selected to grant this wonderful gift to these suffering souls?

*****

Running from the airplane to the small hut, we could see only snow — snow, all around, piled several meters high — and dressed in our scant refugee clothing, feel the bitter cold of the whining Arctic wind. But once inside, we were met by warm and friendly Canadians. Our hosts processed us efficiently through immigration, and then ushered us into the 'lobby'. Here we were greeted by a group of people, including the Mayor of Gander, who had arranged a hospitable reception for these latest additions to the Canadian melting pot. A simple, but filling, meal of vegetable soup heated up from cans labeled "Campbell's" and sandwiches — bologna and thin squares of orange cheese on bread that had the antiseptic consistency of cotton batten — was served, along with some grape juice, with which, in the absence of champagne, our Canadian friends welcomed us to our new homeland — and. of course, lest I forget, toasted the Queen. And this, all at two o'clock in the morning on the day before Christmas![22]

Finally, once the midnight merriment was over — around three AM, according to the clock on the wall — the friendly Newfoundlanders bused us over to the local Air Force base. Here we were taken to some barracks, and directed to bunk beds, on which we gratefully collapsed. What pleasure, to stretch our limbs out between fresh sheets, after ten straight hours on a cramped plane!

*****

The next morning, after a huge meal — our first taste of North American style breakfasts with eggs and sizzling bacon or little sausages, thick pancakes swimming in melted butter and some deliciously sweet, smoky tasting syrup from the maple tree, toasts of the cotton batten-like white bread and watery coffee — we were taken back by bus to the airport. We were told that our plane had been repaired overnight, and we were to continue our journey to Toronto.

We took off in yet another blizzard — with snowflakes, the likes of which we had never seen in Hungary, descending so densely, that it seemed as if a white sheet had been drawn across the window on the outside. After several hours, when we were already itching to arrive at our destination, the pilot came on the loudspeaker and announced that Toronto, as well as Montreal and Quebec City, and for that matter, the entire eastern seaboard of North America, were experiencing impossible weather conditions. We would not be able to land at Malton International Airport[23], nor at any of those other places. Our best bet was to turn back to where we had come from, to Newfoundland, which, miracle of miracles, was now experiencing clear skies.

Fortunately, though, we did not have to go all the way back to Gander. The pilot managed to find a hole in the thick cloud cover over Moncton, in New Brunswick, and he grabbed the opportunity to land. We stayed overnight in a motel — courtesy of the kind inhabitants of Moncton — and continued our journey to Toronto the next day. This time around, we made it to our destination — our final one we hoped — without any problems.

*****

Up until this point, our impressions of our new homeland had been somewhat mixed, but one thing that was sure was that everything was so new and different for us. So far, we had only seen small towns, where most of the buildings were made of wood — something quite unheard of in the part of Europe where we came from. And lots of snow and ice. The people we met had all been very kind and good, but they all seemed so casual and naïve.

Toronto, on the other hand, appeared to be closer in size to the city where we had spent most of our lives — at least, as far as we could determine as the plane circled over the airport. Certainly, once we had landed, we could see that the terminal was bustling with people still departing or arriving for their Christmas holidays. But here, too, there were huge mounds of snow all over the tarmac, and of course, the penetrating cold that Europeans associate with Canada.

After being processed once again by customs and immigration officials — although God only knows that none of us on the airplane had anything either on us or in our meager luggage that was illegal or for which we would have had to pay duty — we were bussed down to a community hall near the corner of Wellesley and Jarvis Streets, where Canadian officials had made preparations to welcome us. Here, there was a reception in our honor, and gifts — dolls and little toy cars — for the children.

We were allowed to contact friends or relatives, and my father called his brother, Gábor[24] — who already knew from Gida bácsi that we were coming to Canada — in Peterborough, a small town near Toronto, and his sister Klára[25] in Montreal, as well as friends who had emigrated from Hungary after the Second World War. Several of these came over to see us at the community hall, bringing gifts for the new additions to the Hungarian community of Toronto.

*****

Later in the evening, Gábor bácsi arrived with a Canadian friend of his who owned a car large enough — a big Studebaker, I think it was — to seat comfortably a family of five plus the driver and another passenger. Gábor bácsi signed a piece of paper and the immigration officials released us. Accustomed as we were to Communist red tape, we could scarcely believe the ease with which we had been finally admitted to our new homeland.

In the dark and warm womb of the car on the way to Peterborough, where we would spend our first two happy years in Canada, I fell asleep to the soft drone of the engine. I dreamt that there was no earth, just a Heaven and a Hell. And we — my entire family — all had angel's wings growing on our backs, and shining halos above our heads. For some reason we could not fathom, we had been mistakenly condemned to Hell. But somehow, in a harrowing and heroic adventure, we escaped through the Portals of Hell — just as the massive Iron Curtain that had opened to let a brief breath of fresh air through was noisily grinding shut again. We floated through limbo to arrive at the Gates of Heaven on Christmas Morning. Here, Saint Peter, who was smoking a big fat cigar and looked like the pictures of Winston Churchill Alfréd bácsi had shown us — Szent Péter, for he must have been Hungarian — sat at a table, messily munching on some white bread, fried eggs and bacon, and admitted us with an ample gesture of his right hand between bites. As we stood there, staring, mesmerized, at the huge golden Gates, I heard Szent Péter swallow noisily and say to us in a deep and gentle voice, "Ah, you must be that Hungarian family. I've heard all about you! I've heard your story. Come on in. Welcome. I'm quite positive that you'll make good citizens of Heaven. Because, unlike most souls I have allowed in here, you have been to Hell. Good luck to you in your new life."

Before we could respond, Szent Péter added, "Oh, I almost forgot! I have a gift for you, a Christmas gift. Open it. Go on, open it!" And he handed us a parcel, all wrapped in gold.

We tore open the package, and inside, to our surprise and happiness, was … Freedom!

This was indeed the best Christmas of our lives.

Thank you, Szent Péter, and all you other angels, thank you for everything.

Read about the Hungarian Revolution and our exciting escape attempts in the earlier parts of the book!

(I added Footnotes to this excerpt to explain context, as some of this is contained in the excluded arts of the book.)

Pathétique, or Famine in Ethiopia Viewed on St. Nicholas' Day

I wrote this poem when we were living in London, on December 6, 1984, St. Nicholas Day, the start of the holiday season in much of Europe, moved by the horrific famine then raging in Ethiopia. Deemed one of the worst humanitarian events of the twentieth century, it caused an estimated one million deaths between 1983 and 1985 according to the United Nations. The fate of these poor people contrasted starkly with our prosperous life in the West and the happy times we were living that Christmas season. The poem was included in my second volume of poetry, ***Sighs and Murmurs****, published by P.R.A. Publishing in 2018.*

Millions of limbs
hang
limply
from bloated torsos,

Yolkless corneas
grope
blindly
from pock-scarred faces,

While we reach
limply
bearing token gifts,

While we stare
blindly
watching mankind die.

An Unexpected Christmas Gift

This is the beginning of my second memoir, ***The Expo Affair****, published under their MiroLand Imprint by Guernica Editions in 2016. This first section of Chapter 1 tells of how, in 1968, when my family was gathered around the table a few days after Christmas, my brother, Peter, brought to my attention an opportunity that I could not pass up: to work as a host in the Ontario Pavilion at Expo '70, the world's fair in Osaka, Japan. The rest of the book is the story of that life- changing adventure, including learning spoken Japanese, forming friendships across cultures, traveling extensively in then emerging Japan and elsewhere in Asia and being approached by three Czechoslovak hostesses to help them defect to Canada during Expo at the height of the Cold War.*

Chapter 1

It was my brother, Peter, who put me up to it.

We were sitting around the table a couple of days after Christmas, exhausted from the protracted festivities. There were a few slices of walnut and poppy seed roll — *'beigli'*— the delicious traditional Hungarian Christmas dessert still left on the family silver platter that had been smuggled out from behind the Iron Curtain the year before by my grandmother, but we had gorged ourselves and had no more room. It had snowed that morning, and it was the holidays, so no one had any urgent reason to get up from the table. We were lingering, and my parents were probing our plans for the summer and beyond.

"There was an announcement stuck on the bulletin board at Western[26]. At Sydenham Hall," Peter said, as he picked up some poppy seed morsels from the tablecloth with his fingertips and put them in his mouth. "For Expo'70, in Japan. You know . . . the world's fair. The Ontario Government is looking for staff for its Pavilion. Hosts and hostesses. It seemed interesting, but it would mean taking a year off from school." My brother was putting out a feeler.

"Peter, you can't do that," my father weighed in immediately. "Next year is your last year of university, and you know how important it is that you get your degree."

"Well . . ." Peter hesitated, knowing he would lose the argument against my father. "I guess I meant it more for Mongi." (Meaning me. This, or its non-diminutive version, Mongol, was the nickname Peter, my cousin, Zsolt, and I had adopted for each other. With great erudition, the summer before, we had erroneously decided that the Magyars were descended from Mongolians, and ever since then, we have called each other "Mongi" or "Mongol" — Mongolian.)

My ears perked up. This could be it; this could be just the solution to my problems, the way to take a break from university. I was in my second year at Harvard, and while I was enjoying the student life, I was lost: I had no idea of what I wanted to be, or even what I wanted to study. I had started as a Biochemistry major the year before but hated Chemistry. I changed to Government, but found Government 101 boring; besides, it was a huge class, and competition was stiff. I then switched to Geology, because I had heard that in the spring break of second year there was a great field trip to the Bahamas to study coral reefs. Just before coming home for Christmas, though, the professor had cancelled the trip, and I knew I wanted out. 'Rocks for Jocks' was not for me, and my life was a mess.

"What did the announcement say, Mongi, do you remember?" I did not want to sound overly excited.

"I don't know exactly, but I can look. That is, if it's still there when I get back."

"Peter, why don't you," my mother said. "Who knows, it could be an interesting opportunity. It's worth looking into, even if nothing comes of it." She had always dreamed of going to Japan, ever since her father — who had been the official doctor of the 1936 Hungarian Olympic team — had hosted his Japanese counterpart in Budapest two years later when she was ten years old. She had told us stories about this physician and his wife, who had seemed so exotic, so kind and polite to her, and had brought such exquisite gifts, that she had always wanted to go to their country to learn more about Japan and its people.

*****

The topic came up again a week after I returned to Harvard, on the regular Sunday evening telephone call with my parents.

My mother had the details. When they drove Peter back to his dorm at the University of Western Ontario in London, on January fourth, she had copied the announcement word for word. She made me write down whom to contact, and what the application process entailed.

It was not until after I discussed the opportunity with my roommate, George, that I became enthusiastic about applying. Perhaps this really would be a fun experience. Plus, it could help me figure out what to do with my life. Weigh that against dropping out for a year, being away from my friends, my budding fencing career and the Harvard social scene. But taking a break from the endless papers, classes and exams would not be such a bad thing. And, I would still come back and finish the four years, so I would not lose out on the experience — it would just be a little different.

I wrote a letter to a Mr. J.W Ramsay, Director, Special Projects and Planning Branch at the Ontario Department of Trade and Development in Toronto. In the letter, I made up reasons why I really wanted the job and why I thought I was well suited for it. I appended my beefed-up résumé and posted it — but not till the next day. I always like to sleep on such life changing decisions.

This is the just the start of this exciting adventure that took me as host in the Ontario Pavilion at Expo '70 to exotic Japan, which was then embarking on an economic boom and emerging on the international scene. A story of youthful exploits, international friendships, wild partying with alcohol, sex and drugs, and a perilous attempt to help three girls from behind the Iron Curtain defect to the West at the height of the Cold War – it is all there, just read the book!

Christmas and afterthoughts

This is another poem from ***Sighs and Murmurs,*** *my second collection published in 2017 by P.R.A. Publishing. I wrote it one Christmastime in Vermont, during one of many wonderful snowfalls.*

Christmas, and crystal snow flecks drop
from an invisible heaven,
(like grains of sand in an hourglass),
vanishing, ghoul-like, on contact
with a cemented over earth:
their descent through the empty night,
too fast and short-lived: (what sorrow,
what pain, when a child dies!) no time,
there is no time for their beauty—
their timeless, infinite beauty—
to blossom and inflame our love.

Only the flakes know their perfection.

How Rudolf's Nose Turned Red

Now for something a little lighter, less serious! This is a hitherto unpublished children's story I wrote some time ago, based on a tale I made up to tell my children one Christmas. I have told it again and again to young ones, including my grandchildren. It was inspired in part by a children's book by Toni de Geretz entitled, ***Louhi, Witch of the North Farm****, that was a favorite of my little ones. In my two-chapter version of the Rudolf story, they particularly love all the "disgusting things" that Kundiga, the witch I created, brews in her cauldron to distribute to the people of Artemia and Grabsville.*

Chapter 1

Once upon a time, many years ago, in the faraway land of Karelia[27], lived the evil witch Kundiga, who simply hated the entire world. In her cave on a mountainside near the village of Artemia, she plotted and planned the vilest acts against decent folk.

Kundiga loved to get on her witch's broom and ride with the wind over Artemia and the nearby city of Grabsville, cackling and flailing her arms, conjuring up an ice-storm here, a tornado there, a flood or an earthquake, causing as much misery as possible.

One snowy St. Nicholas' Day, she sat by her fire brewing her evil witch's broth — adding a toad here, snake guts there, rats' tails, cockroaches, babies' teeth, birds' poo, just as her fancy directed — cackling and salivating, and dreamt up her most wicked deed ever.

Kundiga leapt up from her stool with gusto and landed in a pile of llamas' livers. But she did not lie there long, because she knew she had work to do, and fast. For the night of St. Nicholas' Day is when Santa Claus goes reconnoitering, to see who in the world was good and who was bad — which he needs to know to be able to decide how many presents he will put in his sack to distribute on Christmas Eve.

Kundiga scratched the hairy wart on her nose in glee as she picked out her speediest broom. She clicked with her yard-long, calloused tongue as she put on her warmest rags over her wizened body. She stuck her nose in the cauldron to sniff her brew, then shot out her tongue, the forked tip of which sizzled as it slurped up some of the broth. Kundiga knew the slop was ready, and poured some of the thick liquid into a stinky old cat skin bag. This she tied around her waist, grabbed the broom, and taking a running start, flew out of the cave. Just in time, because she saw Santa's sleigh already etched against the moonlight high above Karelia.

Kundiga beat her broom to make it go faster and faster, and zoomed ever closer to the unsuspecting jolly old elf. She finally caught him just as he arrived above Artemia, flew directly over him, his sleigh and his reindeer, grabbed the cat skin from behind her and emptied the brew on the lead reindeer's nose, with some of the disgusting slop trickling over the rest of the team and Santa himself. The targeted nose immediately started glowing a bright red, and Kundiga knew she was victorious. She yelled at poor Claus, "I've got you, you stinking old windbag." And at the lead reindeer: "Okay, Rudi, you … you pimple-nose, you are my slave now," as she turned toward her cave.

The reindeer she had called by name followed her broom, in spite of himself. Nor could Santa's angry words and cracking whip get him to do anything other than meekly trail Kundiga's flying broomstick.

Cackling and waving her arms in glee, Kundiga led Santa and his reindeer on a roller-coaster ride, up and down, over and through clouds, jerking sideways, dodging in among the trees of the forest, whipping over the crags of the mountains. Many times, poor old Santa was sure he was a goner — the sensitive old dude, he lost his breakfast over the side, and his brand-new hat flew off his head.

Kundiga finally led her entourage through the mouth of her cave; Santa's clothes were in tatters, torn by the branches and the wind, and his face was as pale as his beard. The witch unhitched the reindeer and sent them scurrying down the mountain slope. She picked up the sleigh and hurled it down after the reindeer — down, down it rolled like a giant snowball, until it broke through the ice on the river in the valley below, scaring the fish to death, and finally came to a stop when it jammed between two big rocks underwater.

Kundiga brushed her hands together as she reentered the cave and cackled at the shattered Santa, "Now I will finish with you once and for all, you piece of quivering blubber, and we will finally have an unmerry Christmas and an unhappy New Year!"

Kundiga picked Santa up with her wizened grey hands, squeezing his belly, lifted him high over her head, and with an eerie witch yell, plunked him, head-first into the wicked witch's brew. The cave reverberated as poor old Santa just sizzled up, right down to his belly button, which was still visible above the lip of the cauldron, as were his wildly kicking legs. When the sizzling finally stopped, Santa's under-the-slop burbled yelling, "Help, help! Somebody please help," was just audible above the bubbling of the brew.

After Santa had boiled enough, Kundiga pulled him out, and tied the no longer jolly old elf — whose belly now looked like a pear, the top part of which was all pink and shriveled like the skin of an ancient pig — and stuffed him in a far corner of the cave.

Chapter 2

The next eighteen days, Kundiga spent collecting as many worms, snakes, toads, lizards, rats, mice, spiders, cockroaches, termites and other disgusting things like llamas' livers, pigs' entrails, cows' eyeballs, rotten vulture eggs, etcetera, etcetera, as she could get her hands on. She gathered them all in a big stretchy mammoth skin that she attached to the top of the highest peak in Karelia. These were going to be the presents for the people of Artemia.

Finally, Christmas Eve arrived, and Kundiga doused herself with her rats' pee perfume and put on her ugliest, filthiest rags and picked out her strongest and fastest broom.

"This will be the Christmas to end all Christmases, you old numbskull," she cackled at Santa who was moaning, all tied up in the darkest corner of the cave.

With a running start, Kundiga zoomed out of the cave, toward the mammoth skin floating in the dark sky above Karelia. From below, in the sinister forest, Rudolf saw the old witch and knew in his heart that if he did not do something now, there would never, ever again be a happy Christmas in Artemia. So, with a powerful leap, he took after the witch.

By this time, Kundiga had reached the mammoth skin, and with her calloused, yard-long tongue, she slashed the cord tethering it to the highest mountain top. Kundiga towed the huge bag behind her as she made her way toward Artemia. Rudolf was gaining on her, but he knew he had to be careful, because his nose was still red, and if the witch saw him, she could will him to do whatever she wished. So, he hid behind the mammoth skin — although he almost fainted several times from the awful stench. He had to wait for just the right moment because he would only have one chance to save Christmas. Rudolf also knew he had to be quick and carry out his plan very soon, because once they were over Artemia, the good people would suffer.

The moment arrived just in the nick of time: as the witch slowed down to make a spiraling turn down toward the town, the mammoth skin floated above her head. A quick jerk of his head, and Rudolf slashed open the big bag with his sharp antlers. All the disgusting things in there floated out and down, almost taking Rudolf with them. Kundiga screamed as she was knocked off her broom by a morass of coagulated llamas' livers, pigs' entrails, snakes, spiders, dead rats, etcetera, etcetera. She fell, spinning through the air, and landed in a pile of disgusting things, with more disgusting things falling on top of her until she was totally covered in disgusting things. Within moments, she was smothered to death by the insects, snakes, dead rats, cows' eyeballs, pigs' entrails, llamas' livers, etcetera, etcetera.

Rudolf grabbed the falling witch's broom in the air with his mouth and rushed back to the cave. He untied the half-dead Santa and brushed him off with the magic broom, turning him back into his real self, the jolly old elf. Santa clambered onto Rudi's back, and they set off for the North Pole. Rudolf waved the magic broom, and within seconds they were there.

Santa ordered his elves to load his spare sleigh with all the toys they had made throughout the year, hitched Rudolf and his back-up reindeer to it and set off for Karelia. He spent the entire night delivering toys and presents to the good people of Artemia and Grabsville, singing, "Rudolf, the red-nosed reindeer …" as he flew from house to house.

Just as the sun rose on a fine Christmas morning Santa and his reindeer, led by Rudolf, finished delivering the stuff — not the disgusting stuff prepared by Kundiga, but the wonderful presents he and his elves made all year. Tired but happy, Rudolf led Santa over the pile of disgusting things where Kundiga, the witch, was rotting away, buried under all the llamas' livers, pigs' entrails, dead rats, snakes, insects, etcetera, etcetera. The stink was so horrible that Santa almost fainted as he waved the magic broom over the mound to sweep away all the disgusting, polluting things, and the earth and the air were clean again.

Then Santa, Rudolf and the back-up reindeer — who were no longer back-ups — headed back toward their home at the North Pole, tired but happy.

To this day, Rudolf's nose is still shiny and red, and he wears this sign of distinction with pride, in memory of the day he saved Christmas from the evil witch, Kundiga. And the children of Karelia can be heard singing "Rudolf the red-nosed reindeer …" most days, even though their parents keep telling them that this is just a Christmas carol.

"Rudolf the red-nosed reindeer …"

Christmas Eve twenty-twenty

This poem I wrote at Christmastime in 2020, at the height of the COVID epidemic which so disrupted normal life, not sparing holidays such as Christmas. It was published in ***The Abyss****, my fifth volume of poetry, by Deux Voiliers Publishing in 2022.*

Christmas Eve twenty-twenty is finally here,
I just settled my brains for a long winter's nap,
and alone I wait with great anticipation
for the joyful sound of hooves pawing on the roof,
the dancing and prancing of eight tiny reindeer.

Will our old Saint Nick come down the chimney this year
to bring the presents I asked for in my letter?

Or, instead of biting on the stump of his pipe,
is our dear, chubby and plump, right jolly old elf,
our immuno-compromised, obese Santa Claus
now sucking oxygen from a ventilator
in the ICU of some over-run hospital
somewhere near the North Pole, cared for by his elves,
all infected by the dreaded COVID virus?

Will he survive to perform his act next Christmas?

Opi and the Sidecar Christmas

This is one of my favorite short stories, published in my collection, ***The Mind Spins****, in December 2021, by P.R.A. Publishing. The wonderful tale in all its aspects is a true one, and it tells of one of the last Christmases we had with my father, who, even in his old age, despite everything he had gone through in life, sparkled with laughter and humor. I wrote it partly to bring him to people who did not know him, but also so that those who did know him would not forget this wonderful human being and the joy he brought into our lives. And to chronicle one of the many delightful Christmases we all spent together as a family.*

"You won't believe this, Geza." Peter's voice chuckled on my answering machine. He must have called from their apartment in Budapest. We had just arrived at our house in wintry Vermont from Vienna to celebrate Christmas with our adult children and other family members. Nicholas, our son, was studying at McGill in Montreal and daughter Alexandra was working in New York — they, and my father and two sisters, brother-in-law and sister-in-law and three nieces were all coming to join us for the holidays.

It was very late, and I was tired, so I almost didn't press the "Play" button till the next morning. Peter's was the first message of note on the recorder.

"You won't believe it." His signature *hyuk-hyuk* snigger sounded like a chicken as he pulled himself together for the killer line. "Opi just called to say his suitcase is all packed. You apparently promised to drive up to Toronto on your motorcycle and take him back in the sidecar to Vermont. For Christmas with you all." Another little snort. "Now, in the middle of winter. That's really nice of you, Gez."

My brother was, no doubt, being sarcastic.

"He's ready and waiting," Peter's message continued. "Oh, yes, do make sure he has a hat and scarf, so he doesn't die of cold on the drive."

Yes, I did believe it — anything was possible with my aging father. His imagination had become more vivid and, I hated to say, somewhat demented with time. But even though I was dead tired after flying across the ocean to Logan, then driving up from Boston, I could not help laughing as I relayed the news to Marcia. I could just picture yours truly wearing thick, black-rimmed goggles, peering through the falling snowflakes, tooling along on the interstate highway for nine hours on a motorcycle — never mind that I did not have one and had never even driven one — with my wizened father, better known to his loved ones as Opi, crouched low in the sidecar beside me, goggles poised on his half-frozen nose, icicles of snot hanging from one of the nostrils, all bundled up in a heavy overcoat, with a scarf billowing behind him like Snoopy in the Red Baron cartoon …

An image that has become vividly etched in my mind, even though it is totally fictional.

*****

If you knew my father, perhaps you would understand. What he had said to my brother made sense at some level, as the utterings — or mutterings — of older people often do. Certainly, if you deconstructed Opi's call to Peter, most of the elements of his statement were based in reality.

Throughout his entire life, my father loved to laugh, and this was infectious. He delighted in telling a joke and in having others enjoy it along with him. So, I wouldn't entirely put it past Opi — this could have been just a fast one on Peter and me. To make us laugh with him.

That said, there was more in his comment to Peter than just laughter. Much more.

*****

First of all, the motorcycle with the sidecar.

In his youth, between the wars, my father did own such a vehicle. A BMW R71 with a sidecar, to be exact. And he used to drive it proudly around Budapest and down to Lake Balaton, parading his beautiful young girlfriend, Lily — who, after a whirlwind courtship, became his wife, at age eighteen, marrying the handsome bachelor of twenty-four. Pictures of the lovers show them smiling, standing beside and sitting astride the vehicle with my mother's arms wrapped around his midriff. But I highly doubt that when they went to the several balls during the season, dressed to the hilt in tails and white tie, my mother resplendent in a long gown, it was on the motorcycle and sidecar. Surely my mother's father would have forbidden it!

And who knows, perhaps before he married Lily, my dashing father took other young ladies, too, for a ride in his sidecar, but I would not know about that.

So, at the very least, the motorcycle with the sidecar was real. Just transposed seventy-five or so years in time, four thousand five hundred miles in distance and from pleasant summertime on the hilly roads around Lake Balaton to harsh winter on the Vermont interstate. And I am quite sure my father — who now lived in an old age home in a suburb of Toronto, where we had settled after our arrival as refugees in Canada — had not even seen a motorcycle with a sidecar since those blissful days in Budapest.

But those are just minor details.

*****

As paterfamilias, there was no question that Opi could, and indeed did not hesitate to ask anyone in his family to do his bidding. Never mind that I might have been exhausted after the arduous trip from Vienna to Vermont, perhaps too tired to jump on a rig, drive five hundred miles in the middle of winter to fetch him, turn around and then speed the same distance back on the icy roads.

Of course, I would do it. Wouldn't any loving son?

Although, by necessity, as I was growing up, I had learned always to listen carefully to the advice and requests that came my way from my parents, to take whatever was said on board, but still, in the end, to do whatever I felt was right.

Fortunately, Opi and Omi had come to trust my judgment, certainly by the time I was fully grown.

I could have simply refused to fetch my father in the sidecar, no hard feelings. Indeed, since I did not have access to a motorcycle with a rig, I would have had the perfect excuse.

*****

It, too, was not out of the question that my father may have just finished what he thought was packing his bags when he called Peter. That activity was second nature to him. Throughout his life — especially after my mother passed away — he had always been on the move, traveling the world with his suitcase to seek out friends and family in the most remote places. And the more exotic the destination, the better.

In fact, when I was transferred to London, the very next day after our little family settled into our temporary accommodation in Kensington — which my then employer, the Royal Bank of Canada, paid for while we found something more permanent — my father was there on our doorstep, carry-on suitcase in hand. The children, who were delighted to see their grandfather, ended up having to share a bedroom so we could accommodate our rather inconvenient first guest. But he was Opi, the paterfamilias.

Through one of Peter's friends who owned a travel agency, my father even managed to register himself as a travel agent so he could get all sorts of freebies and discounts on voyages. This was vintage

Opi. Above all, he relished getting deals on everything. Perhaps this reflected his immigrant background, the fact that he and Omi had started over as refugees in Canada with nothing. To his dying days, he kept this trait.

Cruises were his favorite sort of voyage. With his travel agent card, he managed to get substantial discounts on some lines, supposedly to check them and the particular itinerary out for the travel agency's customers. So, one day when Marcia came upon an article in a travel journal that mentioned free cruises for mature single gentlemen, provided that in return they would be ready to dance with the many spinsters on the boat, she immediately thought of Opi. She enthusiastically brought this to his attention, thinking that he would jump at the opportunity, and … she was completely floored by his rather offended response: "But, my dear, I am not a gigolo!"

Several times when we visited Opi in the old age home where he spent his last years, we would arrive to his room only to find a partially packed suitcase open beside his bed, occasionally with half-devoured salami sandwiches, opened containers of yogurt and moldy jars of *Noszlopi,* his favorite Hungarian hot sauce which Peter's wife, Sue, regularly supplied him with, mixed in with his pajamas and unpaired socks and underwear.

Oh, the caprices of getting old!

*****

And ah, yes, Yuletide! By far, Opi's favorite time of year. He would never miss a family Christmas, even if it meant traveling a great distance in an open sidecar in the middle of winter.

That said, our family Christmases were indeed very special. We celebrated, and still celebrate them, the way Opi and his beloved Lily, my mother, used to. With, of course, a few adaptations. (Marcia and I claim these are improvements.)

Even now, it is Christmas Eve that is special for us, just as it is for most Europeans. As it was when the family event used to be at Opi's and Omi's in Don Mills, the Toronto suburb where they had their bungalow. To this day, when Marcia and I are the hosts—as we were that fateful Christmas when I was supposed to fetch Opi in the sidecar — everyone dresses up for the occasion, all the wrapped presents are arranged under the tree, the conifer carefully chosen and set up a few days earlier is bedecked with beautiful hand-carved and blown glass ornaments, the white electric lights replacing the fire-hazard candles of old are lit, and everyone waits expectantly in another room, while the mythical spirit of Christmas (whether the baby Jesus or Santa Claus or Amazon.com has become blurred in our transcultural version) comes to visit to give his, her or its *imprimatur* ...

And then, the ding-a-ling of some bells — now, rung by me, in days gone by, by my father—indicates that it is time for all to enter the living room. The baby Jesus has blessed the event, Santa has gone back up the chimney, and the Amazon drone has delivered all the presents.

Children first, in order of ascending age; their parents next — one of the nieces pushing Opi in the wheelchair — and then the older ones, that is, my generation, for whom the magic of Christmas has changed from the opulence of the gifts and the lights and the decorations to the wonder and warmth of being with loved ones. The lit-up and decorated Christmas tree spreads its warm glow throughout the room, as in the background, carols play, and in the fireplace, crackling flames add to the ambience.

The spell is then broken by someone saying in either a close-to-tears (Opi or one of my sisters) or a somewhat sarcastic (most likely, my son, Nicholas, or yours truly) voice, "Lovely!" as I struggle to find the track for "Silent Night" — or these days, click the Spotify icon on my iPhone — and we delight in singing along, some of us off-key, the more mature ones in the group tearing up with thoughts of loved ones not present, the younger ones eagerly casing out the mountains of colorfully wrapped presents all ready to be opened, piled under the tree.

Mutual hugging and kissing and the wishing of *Merry Christmas!* follow the dying away of the last strains of the carols — for "Silent Night" is always followed by "Oh, Christmas tree." Then, as my brother-in-law Don assumes contorted poses with his enormous camera and rather phallic lens to snap myriads of pictures, I pop open a couple of bottles of Veuve Clicquot, Marcia and my sister Clara bring in platters of shucked Malpeque oysters, garlic shrimp on sticks, and little toasts spread with chunks of *foie gras mi-cuit.*

While those of us approaching or exceeding the drinking age clink glasses, those palpably younger attack the piles of presents until one of the oldies brings order to the gift giving and opening. It is formally declared that the youngest will start with a present for him or her from under the tree, and then he or she will choose one randomly from the pile and hand it to its intended recipient, aided of course by the order demanding oldie (usually Marcia or my sister Clara).

And so on, until amidst delighted *oohs* and *ahhs* and the occasional *thank you* and kiss of gratitude, all the presents have been distributed to their rightful owners and I have more or less managed to collect the torn wrapping paper and packaging in a garbage bag, or used some of it to stoke the fire, vainly trying to save any somewhat intact pieces and lengths of colorful ribbon for future Yuletides.

After several declarations that this has been the "best Christmas ever", the ladies in the group repair *en masse* to the kitchen to bring to the beautifully set dining table the delicacies prepared earlier for the Christmas Eve meal. I fetch the wine, a St. Émilion Grand Cru opened earlier for the red, an Entre Deux Mers straight from the fridge for white — while Opi and my sister Susan surreptitiously stuff the remaining *hors d'oeuvres* into their mouths and Alexandra and Nicholas and the cousins race to down the unfinished contents of dangerously poised champagne *flûtes.*

After I point out my reserved seat at one corner, everyone finds their place and the noise of scraping chairs is punctuated by the now repetitive and somewhat boring *oohs* and *aahs*. In the middle of the linen tablecloth, in pride of place, sits a cold poached salmon procured the day before and prepared in the morning with much love by Marcia, skin carefully peeled off, and meticulously decorated with slivers of red peppers, olives and dill greens, to be consumed with a cold cucumber sauce. Alongside the fish platter, on separate serving dishes, are thin slices of prosciutto San Daniele and Csabai, a spicy Hungarian sausage, as well as an array of Vermont cheeses augmented with Société Roquefort and Comté from France, a quinoa salad speckled with pomegranate pips, seedy and multigrain iterations of my homemade bread and various condiments. Everyone digs in; no one, not even my niece who is usually a rather selective eater, holds back. Opi proves that he still has a healthy appetite, at least for the delicious homecooked Christmas meal Marcia has masterminded. Much wine is consumed — indeed I have to go back down to the cellar for a third bottle of the St. Émilion.

But the *pièce de résistance* comes at the end. For dessert is an Austro-Hungarian specialty that has been refined over the many centuries of Habsburg rule, yet each iteration is unique. Mine is a version of my mother's. She, it must be said, could have been a master chef, certainly for pastries, not just at Gundel's in Budapest, but any Michelin-starred restaurant. The delicacy is known as *beigli* in Hungarian and for Opi, as it is now for all of us, no Christmas is complete without it. And the "it" needs to be home baked.

De rigueur, there must be two kinds of beigli: one filled with a ground poppy seed stuffing, the other made with freshly ground walnuts. But it is not as simple as that. The poppy seed for the filling has to be finely ground to release the rich, flavorful oils. The paste is then usually combined with melted butter and varying amounts of sugar — I replace the sugar with Vermont maple syrup (actually, also in my walnut filling) — raisins soaked overnight in rum, zested organic lemon and a touch of apricot jam or grated apple. The walnut one is similarly doctored with like additives. The concoction is rolled in a pastry made with lots of butter and eggs and baked until golden brown. The key to the art of beigli baking is that the pastry should be as invisible as possible, yet still hold the rolls together. Best served with a Tokaji Aszu 6 Puttonyos or Tokay Esszencia, my father always said. In a pinch, Chateau d'Yqem or even a Trockenbeerenauslese will do.

After dinner, while the hosting team cleans up with the help of those who can still move and are so inclined, the members of the younger set inspect their gifts and show them off to Opi and to each other. Then some games — these days, it's usually Celebrity, introduced to the family by Alexandra during her college days — accompanied by a selection of brandies, *pálinkas*, *slivovitzes* and other *eau de vies*, and perhaps tangerines and chocolates for those who favor a healthier postprandial treat.

As the fire turns to embers and the energy of even the youngest starts to ebb away, some members of the group say good night and peel off with kisses all around. Opi, too, decides that he should finally turn in on this loveliest of Christmas Eves.

*****

The next day, of course, we always do the Christmas morning thing with stockings on the mantelpiece for the wee ones (I sometimes attach a dirty sock alongside for fun, hoping against all hope that the more secular Santa or at least Amazon, if not the baby Jesus, will indulge me …), so we do combine the European with the North American way of celebrating Yuletide. And for the main midafternoon meal, Marcia prepares a delicious turkey with foie gras and chestnut stuffing that is to die for, and the beigli is served up again for dessert. Indeed, it remains the dessert of choice for at least ten days after the celebrations, until all the pastry is consumed, and the last crumbs are deemed too dry for human consumption.

*****

It was for such a family Christmas that Opi wanted me to fetch him in the sidecar. As it was, we did not have to resort to such desperate measures. He flew to a nearby airport with my sister Susan, who also lives in Toronto, and met up with my other sister Clara and her husband Don, who arrived at a similar hour from Chicago.

The sidecar Christmas was one of our last times with Opi, and one that we will all cherish fondly. As we treasure all our memories of this wonderful man, who so deeply loved and marked each and every one of us.

My father passed away on June 28, 2011, at age 89. May he rest in peace.

The Nutcracker

My family just loves the ballet, ***The Nutcracker****, and it has become a holiday tradition for a group of us to go to it each Christmas whenever possible. My daughter, Alexandra, danced for many years, and especially bonded with Clara, the little girl central to the ballet. I wrote this poem after seeing a wonderful performance in San Francisco and it was published in my fourth collection,* ***Extinction Rebellion****, in 2020 by Cyberwit.net, an Indian publisher.*

It's Christmas Eve, a roaring fire,
but instead of Clara's dream world
of Drosselmeier's Nutcracker
who defeats a rodent army
led by the Mouse King in battle,
then turns into a handsome prince
to take her to the Land of Sweets
ruled by the Sugar Plum Fairy,
my dream is of a healthy world,
a world where we can breathe clean air
and drink unpolluted water,
where we all get enough to eat,
where civilians are not bombed
and there is no war, no killing—
but I know there is no such world
and there never will be again.

One Christmas and its Turkey

***One Christmas and its Turkey** is a hitherto unpublished story I wrote in the summer of 2024, looking back at the previous Christmas. This was a holiday when my sister, Clara's family and mine, all got together, and we enjoyed lots of activities and meals together around the celebrations. The traditional Christmas Day one was particularly memorable, as the story tells. It was as I started writing **One Christmas and its Turkey**, that I got the idea to create this little volume, bringing together all my works that touched upon this festive time of the year, Yuletide.*

I. Planning

Planning for our Christmases usually starts early in the year. First, always comes the question of where the celebrations will take place: our main residence in rural Vermont, in San Francisco where our daughter, Alexandra, lives with husband, David, and their two little boys, and where we have a small apartment, or in Nairobi, Kenya, where we have our son, Nicholas, and his lovely Hungarian wife, Fanni, with our two little granddaughters. The planning of course assumed that our immediate family – Marcia and me, our daughter Alexandra and her family of four, and Nicholas and his – will celebrate together. The issue of place, however, is usually tied up with who will participate, and what other alternative family pressures weigh on the next generation.

For example, Fanni's family also seeks to gather all its immediate members together for holidays, usually in Budapest, where they live, or perhaps somewhere skiing in neighboring Austria. This is not really an issue with our son-in-law, David, because he and Alexandra, as part of their wedding vows, promised each other that they would always spend

Thanksgiving with his family and Christmas with ours. So far, this arrangement has worked well.

Then, there is the question of whether to open joint Christmas celebrations up to the wider family. Of course, Diane, Marcia's only sister, who is without children, is regularly included, but she always leaves husband Bob behind because he prefers to avoid broader family get-togethers, especially those with wee ones. Also then, should any of my siblings be asked, with their offspring and the grandchildren? Especially my sister, Clara, whose three daughters are very close to my two children, as are the members of the even younger generation of these families. Including my brother Peter and his family would have brought the numbers up to thirty-six, and it is unlikely that they would all assemble to join us since airline fares are expensive at that time of year and travel can be difficult.

But the particular Christmas in question, this all fell in place very nicely. Early on, Clara declared that they could celebrate in San Francisco, since daughter Jenny, who also lives there and her new French boyfriend, Mikael, would, in the course of the following year be taking off on a trans-Pacific crossing in a catamaran, and she was ruing the fact that she would not see her daughter for at least a year – if ever, she confessed to us, she could not help thinking sometimes in the night – and that certainly, it would be wonderful to say good-bye to them before they took off on such an extended voyage. Theresa, her oldest daughter jumped on the wagon almost immediately, as she and husband, Mike, were always keen on bigger family gatherings, and San Francisco held a particular soft spot in her heart. With the Golden Gate City rapidly becoming the leading candidate for a broader family celebration, Alexandra – and we, of course – suggested that we should have joint celebrations.

For Nicholas and Fanni, who would have to travel the farthest and do so with two little daughters, it was a bit more of a difficult decision, but they are always game to see the cousins, especially when they can break the trip from Nairobi up by traveling via Hungary (where Fanni's family lives) both ways, and of course, when parents help with the finances. Stephanie, Clara's middle daughter, who would have to fly with husband Adam and two little children from London, would also have to overcome some complications and they too faced a long flight. Moreover, they would no doubt want to see what else they could tie in with traveling all the way to San Francisco.

Alexandra was delighted, although it was obvious that she and David would be hosting most of the largescale gatherings, not least because they had the biggest house there among all of us. Fortunately, their place in Pacific Heights is spacious enough to hold gatherings even of the twenty-three of us – yes, that was the number Marcia came up with when she finally counted the likely attendees on her fingers. As for accommodations, it was assumed from the get-go that Nicholas, Fanni, Sophia and Lara would stay with Alexandra and David and cousins Sebastian and Orlando in their large house in Pacific Heights, and Diane with us in our small apartment on Russian Hill. Jenny and Mikael would be at their own one-bedroom place, which, fortunately, was right in between ours and Alexandra's, while Clara, in her usual zealously organized fashion, managed to find a place in the Marina via AirBnB almost immediately after the decision, not too far away, to accommodate the remaining ten members of her immediate family.

Once the issues of 'who' and 'where' are resolved in this early planning stage, *de rigueur* the next big question that immediately comes up for our family gatherings is food and its companion, drink. Since, over the years, we have established a tradition for how we do Christmas – much of it derivative from the way my parents used to hold these family holiday celebrations – there was usually very little variation. The main event, of course, is always Christmas Eve, as it is in Hungary, and indeed, much of Continental Europe.

This dinner is always cold. And it is usually preceded, as the presents are opened, by Champagne, to accompany *foie gras* on thinly sliced fresh baguette, Marcia's smoked trout dip on rice crackers, and when possible, oysters or crab or some other seafood delicacy. David and Alexandra decided early on that this time, this latter delight would be caviar from a high-end specialty shop near them. David also undertook to provide a fabulous vintage Veuve Clicquot Grande Dame to go with the *hors d'oeuvres.*

As the tradition has evolved over the years, the main course for Christmas Eve has become a delicious poached salmon prepared by Marcia, served cold with her out-of-the-world cucumber sauce, but as the number of the eventual attendees crystallized at twenty-three, it became obvious that this might be too difficult a task, even for my master hostess and chef wife, and we collectively decided that we would have to deviate by instead barbequing several sides of salmon. David again kindly volunteered, declaring that "Of course. That makes sense, and I'm happy to do it." The cucumber sauce, fortunately, was not dropped – Marcia would only have to concoct a much larger quantity of it.

Alongside the salmon, she usually conjures up a quinoa salad with pomegranate seeds and other yummy ingredients, and Clara and Jenny jumped in to take that on as their task along with a green salad. Served usually are also prosciutto San Daniele, some sausages or salami, and favorite local cheeses along with Société Roquefort and Comté, aged if it can be found. David again took on the enjoyable responsibility of finding appropriate accompanying wines in his copious cellar.

With only a few years hiatus after my mother passed away, dessert for Christmas Eve has become my job. The main yuletide dinner-ending delicacy is Hungarian *beigli*: this usually consists of at least two baked dough rolls, one with ground poppy seed filling, the other one with ground walnut. These ground bases are usually cooked a little in some water or milk, and I have come to augment the fillings with a sweetener of Vermont maple syrup and raisins soaked in rum, as well as grated lemon peel and apricot jam. The key to success is to roll the dough out so it is as thin as possible, yet not so that it will split once baked. A glaze of egg yolk helps but does not assure that the roll will hold together. Making beigli always ends up being a bit of a game of chance. Additional sweets are usually vanilla crescents and rum chocolate balls – that is, if there is the will and the time to prepare these as well. My mother left us wonderful recipes for both of these delicacies.

Over the years, for joint Christmases like this one, Don, Clara's husband, has jumped into the beigli baking game to compete with at least one roll, usually a walnut one. Indeed, several times he has managed to show me up, although when finally consumed, usually no one dares to pick a winner, declaring each delicious and beautiful in its own way. For dessert too, David would find an appropriate wine in his cellar to accompany these delicacies.

Once the menu for Christmas Eve has been decided, the question of what to consume for brunch the next morning is an easy one, with scrambled eggs and bacon to be served, as pursuant to Anglo-Saxon tradition, Santa's down-the-chimney escapade is celebrated and the stockings hanging on the mantlepiece are attacked by the bambini in the separate sibling family get-togethers.

And then, once again, we get to the joint dinner for all twenty-three of us, this time for Christmas Day. In keeping with American and Canadian custom, we pretty well always have opted for turkey with potatoes – for the more health-conscious, sweet potatoes – done some way and a green vegetable, such as Brussels sprouts or broccoli. Marcia has a delicious stuffing of *foie gras,* chestnuts and shiitake mushrooms she struggles to insert under the skin and into the gaping cavity, and of course, this time, she took on the entire task of dealing with the beast from ordering it to roasting it. She planned to enlist the trusted help of sister Diane in the stuffing preparation. David assured us that his cellar has ample quality wine to serve with the holiday bird and its *accoutrements*.

And, since I am almost always accused of making way too much beigli, this delicious dessert continues to be served up for evening meals during the entire celebratory season until it is all consumed or deemed too dry or moldy to serve. Dessert, as for all meals during the holiday season would be beigli and the other little cookies.

The question of the menus having been settled, next the ladies – particularly Clara, Marcia, Theresa and Alexandra – exchanged numerous emails on the format for the gift exchange. It was decided, after many back-and-forth rounds and false starts, that there would be a draw, whereby each person would be randomly assigned the name of one of the other attendees and be responsible for procuring a gift of fifty dollars or less for the selected person. To make this latter task easier, everybody was tasked with providing a list of two or three items they would prefer as gifts. Parents of the little children would, of course, take on both these responsibilities on behalf of their offspring.

II. The Lead Up

As the holiday family event approached, excitement in all quarters grew apace. Especially the grandchildren's generation could hardly wait to see their cousins and second cousins. And, of course, what gifts Santa and the baby Jesus, or more mundanely for those less believing, their parents or other relatives, would leave for them under the Christmas tree and in their stockings the next morning.

Regarding the all-important nutritional elements, Marcia made calls to Marina Meats well ahead of the feast to make sure that they would have a twenty-five pound turkey for us – and, since they told her they would only be able to procure a frozen one, that they would be able to let it thaw out in time for us to pick up on the Saturday, as Christmas Day fell on the following day. Also, a call to Costarella Seafoods, the fresh fish wholesaler in the Marina we had come to frequent since they were prepared to sell to retail customers on the side, for cash, provided one ordered at least a pound of fish or seafood. The quantity was not a problem for us this time, since we figured that the twenty-three healthy appetites we would be catering to, would have no trouble consuming at least eight or nine pounds of barbequed salmon.

A week or so before the big day, Alexandra and David went out to buy a Christmas tree. My daughter tracked me down on my iPhone from the parking lot temporarily used for the sale of the trees to get my thoughts on the required height: the living room in their four-story house had lofty ceilings, but she could not remember how high. We agreed that a ten-foot spruce would do the job and still accommodate the straw angel in peasant attire we had acquired when we lived in Vienna to decorate our *Tannenbaum* then.

Once the tree was procured, a few nights before the arrival of the first out-of-town guests, Marcia and I went over to help with the job – or indeed, pleasure – of decorating the tree. David had brought up the boxes of ornaments, lights and other paraphernalia from the garage, and these were duly opened. My task was always to first unwrap the clingy plastic netting draped around the tree and then to put on the lights. These chores were never easy, especially on such a monster sapling, but taking my time, and listening to unnecessary admonitions from my wife and daughter not to fall off the step stool, I managed to wrap the three strings of miniscule white lights around the tree. Then, Sebastian and Orlando – choreographed by Marcia, and joined eventually by Alexandra – swooped in to decorate the lower and middle boughs of the tree, while I, as the tallest, and the person by now used to the heights of the step stool, was charged with putting the straw doll on top, and then the many little angels and birdies and other ornaments on the upper reaches. This was all performed to the first strains of Christmas music – I particularly asked for Bach's *Christmas Oratorio* – and a flûte or two of bubbly to wet the drying throats of the adults, and some 'kiddie wine,' as Sebastian and Orlando dubbed it, for the children. All in all, the tree was deemed beautiful and the decorating exercise a success.

Except for an argument right at the end about the covering for the stand and the floor around the tree. Now, we had always used a traditional Hungarian greyish linen tablecloth, beautifully embroidered with red ornamentation, that my grandmother had given us some years back. For whatever reason, Alexandra – acquiesced by Marcia – argued that we should cut it on one side along the radius right to the middle so it could be just pulled over the stand and the surrounding floor and rested snugly against the tree trunk. I duly reminded them that we had always just folded and wrapped it around in whatever way to cover the unsightly wooden cross or metal contraption that held the tree erect without compromising the integrity of the table covering. For some reason, this was no longer acceptable to the ladies, so after duly voicing my preference, and declaring what a travesty it would be to cut the beautiful tablecloth, I ultimately gave in to the desecration of that particular item of my Hungarian heritage. In the end, I consoled myself that this was a piece brought out only once a year, and then amply covered over with gifts for a good part of the time it was in evidence.

Over the next couple of days, the presents started to appear under the tree and the Hungarian tablecloth did indeed disappear. Sebastian and Orlando occasionally sauntered over to shake one or two of the wrapped packages that sported tags with their names to try and guess what was inside, and once a day, Sebastian mastered the task of pouring water from a jug into the stand without wetting too many of the beautifully wrapped gifts. The primary focus of at least the adults though, returned to planning the events and especially the meals.

The far-flung members of the family were expected over the next few days, and Marcia and I awaited with keen anticipation the arrival of Nicholas and Fanni, Sophia and Lara. The day before they were to leave from Budapest, we learned that Nicholas had tested positive with COVID, probably catching the infection from his daughters and Fanni who they admitted had been sick the week before but would no longer be infectious when they arrived. There was some consternation about the risk Nicholas would pose for the other Christmas celebrants, but we all agreed that it would be a shame if he and his little family did not come. Nicholas, though, would have to isolate himself and wear a mask for all the events, at least for the first few days. Alexandra agreed that they could still stay at their place despite this unpleasant new development, but he would have to spend most of the time upstairs in the guest "suite", joining in any celebrations fully masked and at least the requisite six feet away. Nevertheless, when they finally did arrive and I drove out in David's car to pick them up, there was much happiness all around as we hugged the little ones and sent Nicholas kisses from far away, even as he repaired upstairs.

Clara and her family members announced their arrival in due course. Marcia, Alexandra, Clara and Jenny had prepared many memorable events and excursions for all or part of the twenty-three-member group, such as an outing to the Discovery Museum in Sausalito and a late birthday party for Sophia who turned five on December 20th with an elaborate strawberry cake that masqueraded as the dress for a Barbie doll conjured up by Marcia and Diane – truly a work of art. While all these occasions were indeed memorable in their own right, the focus here must be kept to the Christmas celebratory events.

So, Saturday morning, Marcia and I walked down to the Marina to pick up the salmon at Costarella Seafoods and I carried it in my backpack straight to Alexandra's. We then drove with her entire family ceremoniously to Marina Meats to fetch the turkey and some bacon for the filling to take back to their place. The bird was not cheap – I was surprised, when with the bacon, the credit card charge came to $204. Back in the car, the turkey poised all the way in the rear beside Orlando, we were keen to get it into their fridge, although Marcia expressed her concern that it would not be able to fit. Alexandra reassured her that she would be able to make room enough for the beast. To add to all the chaos and excitement, on the trip home, Sebastian accused Orlando of farting, to which Alexandra's comment was "You guys ..."

III. Christmas Eve

The twenty-fourth finally arrived, and for the morning, Jenny and Mikael had planned a treasure hunt for the children on appropriately named Treasure Island, where he was involved with an engineering firm building a residential and commercial complex. This only heightened the excitement for the little ones as we told them that it was essential we were all away from Alexandra and David's house where the baby Jesus and / or Santa were at work with the final arrangements for Christmas.

We all met in the Marina, from where a boat took us over to the island. Mikael and Jenny went ahead leading the troop of little ones first into the old Naval Base, where his office was, and then on a march to various parts of the island, stopping here and there where they had hidden some "treasure" – chocolate gold coins and other goodies and cheap trinkets. The outing was deemed a major success by all the participating children and parents, but for different reasons.

We had resolved to assemble early for the evening's celebrations – at four in the afternoon – everyone dressed to the hilt, even as late-arriving wrapped presents surreptitiously appeared under the tree. To start the proceedings, everyone repaired upstairs, while I, the self-appointed Master of Ceremonies, made a last-minute inspection, plugging in the Christmas lights, adjusting a few presents in the pile and turning on the strains of *Silent Night.* Once satisfied, I rang the shiny brass bell we had brought over from our place, signaling that Santa and the baby Jesus had finished all the preparations, and the family hordes were allowed to make their appearance.

Sebastian, Orlando, Brady, Vivian and Sophia tripped over each other as they ran down the stairs with gleaming expectation in their eyes, while a puzzled little Lara clung to Fanni and Stephanie guided Olivia down the step\s, with Adam carrying Lucas. The smiling and kibbitzing adults followed, and once all twenty-three of us crowded around the tree, we hugged and kissed, wishing each other a "Merry Christmas", even as the children started to rummage through the pile of presents.

We then gathered around the piano, where Sebastian played his *fortissimo* version of *Silent Night* as the adults sang along, some beautifully, others like me who were tone deaf, out of tune. Alexandra brought out the previously prepared *hors d'oeuvres* – the caviar and the *fois gras* – while David popped open the Champagne. The adults "oohed" and "aahed" over these delicacies, even as Marcia – who took over the role of Master of Ceremonies – instructed Sebastian to initiate the doling out of the presents as per the previous agreement of how this would be done. After Sebastian read the name of the recipient of the first gift, then that person tore the wrapping paper off whatever object, breaking away only as he or she was instructed to select the next one from the pile and deliver it to its recipient – and so on, until all the packages were gone. I assumed my role of collecting the hastily shredded wrapping paper, salvaging any nicer pieces and ribbons deemed reusable, frequently interrupting this task to look at the presents being doled out and to lubricate myself with a swig from my champagne flûte.

With all the gifts distributed to the greater or lesser appreciation of the recipients, the ladies determined that it was time to bring out the main dishes for the evening meal – the barbequed salmon, the cucumber sauce, the salads, the cold cuts and the cheeses. These were served up buffet style, with the mothers of the wee ones first serving their children at a separate table. Then came the three bigger boys on their stools at the kitchen counter, with the sumptuous remainders left for the rest of us to politely fight over. As always, there was more than enough to go around, and, of course, the adults made a serious dent in David's wine cellar.

The main course finished, it was time to serve the beigli. For me, the poppy-seed roll is always the highlight of the Christmas meal, and its yumminess was enhanced by the Chateau d'Yqem David served with it, even though this was a significant departure from the Tokay Six Puttonyos or Tokay Esszencia usually served with this delicacy. A fruit bowl helped ease the decadence for the more calorie conscious.

Soon after dinner, amid profuse expressions of gratitude for "the best Christmas ever", most of the Jurivich clan peeled off to put the little ones to bed, as no doubt with Santa filling stockings and clambering down chimneys, the next morning would be an early one, once again bringing much excitement. The children residing in the Farber household were quickly ushered off to bed as well, even as those adults not engaged in this activity made greater or lesser attempts to help with the cleanup while continuing to sip on the remains of the Sauternes or subsequently offered digestifs such as Cognac or a Single Malt.

Marcia and I took our leave after the cleanup and the usual discussion of what a wonderful Christmas Eve we had all enjoyed together with the Juris, deciding to walk home since we all agreed that we were unlikely to be mugged on the way as it was still a reasonable hour and Christmas Eve.

IV. Christmas Day and the Turkey

Christmas morning arrived, and Marcia and I made our way over to Alexandra's for brunch, arriving only after the four little ones had emptied their stockings. They were early risers, and of course, with the excitement of the possibility of finding gifts from a Santa Claus – whose existence and expected journey down the chimney was vehemently denied by our rational oldest grandson, Sebastian, but fervently believed in by the other three younger grandchildren – there was no way we could get there in time. Nevertheless, when we arrived, the little ones bombarded us with a "show and tell" of all the presents they had found, and clever little Sophia even pointed to a disturbance of the fireplace tools – rearranged by David as he and Alexandra were filling the stockings – as evidence that Santa did indeed come down the chimney during the night with a bag of gifts. I pointed out that he must have ascended coughing up a storm and filthy from the ashes from the firep the night before, but agreed that she probably would not have been able to hear his hacking since she was sleeping all the way upstairs.

The plan then was for the men – that is, David, Nicholas and me to take the children to the park, where we would meet up with the some of the Juris – while Alexandra set the table and toiled on other last-minute preparations, and Marcia and Diane got to work on the turkey, first stuffing it and then putting it in the oven. After all, a twenty-five-pound beast would require at least four and a half, possibly five hours of roasting. Preparing the rest of the meal would be relatively easy – cut up potatoes and brussels sprouts all on the barbecue, salad for the vegetarians especially in Clara's family, plus all the starters. Mikael, Jenny's partner, had promised that he would bring fresh crab, caught by his team at work on their annual pre-Christmas crabbing party.

Dealing with the turkey was always a slimy and icky job. First, the stuffing had to be prepared – the foie gras appropriately enhanced with cognac and other goodies, then mixed with the breadcrumbs, herbs, chestnuts and finally the shiitake mushrooms. Once ready, the skin of the turkey needed to be raised off the breasts, and the stuffing inserted underneath, as well as inside the cavity. A slimy, rather unpleasant job.

It took both Marcia and Diane to lift out the beast from the fridge, unwrap it and then start to work on it. As they did so, they both recounted afterwards, they were struck by the somewhat pungent, unpleasant odor that emanated from the animal, but ascribed it just to the usual smell of raw meat. Once they triumphed with the stuffing job, they hoisted the bird on the roasting pan into the appropriately preheated oven, complimenting themselves on a difficult task successfully carried out.

It was only when we returned from the park with the children, and David drew attention to the stench of rotten eggs, a disgusting sulfur-like odor that permeated the entire house, that collectively – after some vehement discussion nevertheless – we took the decision that it could only be emanating from the turkey the ladies had so gallantly stuffed, which must have gone bad and could not be served. Especially to the entire extended family on Christmas Day!

What to do? How were we going to feed twenty-three mouths, some (like Mike, Nicholas, Sebastian and Brady) bigger eaters than others, on such a holiday? It was clear, though, that the offending turkey would not do. Ending up with several Christmas celebration attendees violently sick would be the wrong kind of memory to be left with.

David came to the rescue yet again. Checking the time on his phone, he said, "I will run over to Mollie Stone's. I know they are still open and no doubt they will have something." A nearby up-scale grocery store that he frequented, could be our holiday saver.

Alexandra piped up, "Yes, maybe you can get flank steak or something." A replacement turkey was out of the question – Marcia did not want to have anything to do with a representative of that species ever again, moreover, this late in the game the bird would never have enough time to get done.

While David rushed out to Mollie Stone's before it closed early on Christmas Day, I was tasked with taking the smelly, partially baked turkey out of the oven. There was a brief discussion among the ladies as to whether we should somehow keep it to take back to Marina Meats the next day they opened, to prove that they had sold us a rotten foul fowl, or whether we should chuck it in the compost. I was chastised for jokingly suggesting that we could give it to the homeless as an alternative to the original intention of risking twenty-three of our family members' lives. As punishment for the sick levity, the ladies ordered me to take the steaming stinky beast out and dump it in the green composting bin.

So, I put on a pair of oven mits, grabbed the two sides of the weighed down piping hot pan and, as the grandchildren were told to get out of the way, ceremoniously carried it out the front door, down the steps, taking a sharp right to where the garbage bins were kept. As Marcia propped the lid of the garbage can open, I tilted the pan so that the juicy bird could just slide into the filth with a satisfying thud as it hit bottom. Stuffing, juices and all. There went two hundred and four dollars' worth of solid protein, plus close to another hundred for the *fois gras*, chestnuts and mushrooms, I thought to myself. As I performed this act, I pictured in my mind the surprise of the garbage man the following collection day when he came across the half-roasted twenty-five-pound animal, there naked with all the other food scraps. No doubt it would be a sight to behold.

To conclude the saga of the Christmas Day dinner *sans dinde*, David returned from Mollie Stone's with a huge flank steak which, when all were assembled for the meal again, he barbequed beautifully. Everyone except the staunch vegetarians delighted in it, and there were many declarations such as, "Much better than any turkey." To which I added, *sotto voce*, "Certainly than a rotten one!" Marcia again declared that she would never again deal with a turkey, especially not a frozen one.

The meal was a success, thanks to David's quick response and no doubt the delicious wines he conjured up from his cellar also helped make a difference. Even my, and Donald's, beiglis were ecstatically appreciated, especially as this time around, we served the appropriate Tokay Aszu Six Puttonyos that Fanni and Nicholas had brought all the way from Hungary.

To conclude this rotten fowl tale, on the Tuesday morning following Christmas, Marcia and I hightailed it to Marina Meats – without the offending beast – and complained that they had sold us a turkey gone bad and related the entire story of how it came close to spoiling Christmas for our entire family of twenty-three. The Manager was called and, of course, he was very apologetic, telling his staff member to immediately refund the two hundred and four dollars to my credit card.

Although we were more or less financially whole (minus of course the wasted expensive stuffing ingredients) and delighted that this Christmas ended up as a success, nevertheless, it was difficult to get the bad odor of a rotten turkey and an almost spoiled Yuletide out of our system. But over time, the memory has turned into just one more that we only look back on with a smile, and an episode to laugh about whenever the participants get-together.

Let's ring in the New Year ...

(New Year's Eve, 2020)

I wrote this poem at the end of 2020, a year that brought a lot of suffering and destruction around the world: the COVID pandemic, then wildfires, drought, torrential rains, flooding and violent storms caused or aggravated by climate change, wars and famine and increasing poverty and disparity in the distribution of wealth in many parts of the world. (Clearly, a lot more suffering than that caused by a turkey gone bad!) The poem is one of hope that we can turn this around and create a better world. It was published in ***The Abyss,*** *my fifth collection, by Deux Voiliers Publishing in 2022.*

Let's ring in the New Year with glee
and banish this one with no tears:
it brought such pain, so many deaths
suffering and uncertainty,
poverty caused by the virus,
people left homeless by climate,
by wildfires, floods and hurricanes,
the ugly voice of extremists,
the deaths of brothers and sisters
killed by those meant to protect them,
the rich, of course, getting richer
the poor only poorer, each day—

Let's ring in the New Year with hope:
vaccines to defeat the virus,

a brand-new administration
that cares for the people it serves,
the environment they live in,
the future they and their children have,
clean air to breathe, water to drink,
and unpolluted food to eat—

Let's ring in the New Year and work,
hold hands to build a better world!

Christmas in Vermont (Epilogue from *Twisted Fates*)

The following is from the last book in my ***'Twisted'*** *trilogy,* ***Twisted Fates****, published in 2018 by Black Opal Books. The first book in the series,* ***Twisted Reasons****, starts off in Vienna (where I lived when I began to write it, very much inspired by Graham Green's* ***The Third Man*** *and the eponymous movie). It is the story of two Hungarian American friends, one of whom – Adam Kallay, an employee of the International Atomic Energy Agency – gets involved with Russian 'merchants of evil' in a heist of some nuclear material from the site where Stalin's scientists developed the Soviet atomic bomb. His childhood friend and college roommate, Greg Martens (somewhat modeled on me), finds out about this when he goes to visit in Vienna, and the rest of the book is about Greg's efforts to get to the bottom of the heist. The two sequels,* ***Twisted Traffick*** *and* ***Twisted Fates****, see him pursue these same merchants in other criminal activities such as human, drug and arms trafficking. The* ***Epilogue*** *has Greg and his second wife, Julia, reminiscing, as they are celebrating one Christmas Eve in Vermont where they have settled as older adults, about their exciting earlier exploits.*

Christmas in Vermont was always magical, and everyone in the family loved the time together. But none more than Greg and Julia, for whom having son, Adam, and daughter, Anne, with her husband George, and their children Andrew and Lily, there together at their home, was always a time to be cherished. As every year, they opened the presents *en famille,* before dinner on Christmas Eve with the tree lit, sipping champagne to accompany little *tartines* of *foie gras*, oysters, and skewers of shrimp in front of a roaring fire.

The last gift left under the tree was one wrapped in burgundy-colored paper and tied with gold ribbon, the same shape and size every year. The entire family had come to know full well that the package contained a delicious Sachertorte in a wooden box from Greg's and Julia's friends, the Labrecques, who were now living in Paris, but it had never been fully explained to them who these people were, and why they would be sending a present. The same thing every year. The iconic Viennese gift, a Sachertorte. Each Christmas, the grandparents had sloughed it off, saying, "Oh, one day you will meet them. They are great people, and we did some interesting stuff together. Remember, Andrew, we talked about the heist of nuclear material — you read about it in *Twisted Reasons,* remember. We first knew the Labrecques in Vienna, from where Sachertorte comes." Greg usually added something like, "Yes, I used to stay at the Hotel Sacher, right opposite the opera. One day we will all go and see a performance there and stay at that hotel — it is beautiful — and eat lots of Sacher torte. You will love it."

This year though, Lily would not let it go. "Grandma, you have got to tell us why you keep getting this gift — this cake — every year from these same people. The same present every year. Why?"

Julia hesitated a moment, then looking at Greg, who nodded, answered, "Well, Lily, and Andrew, you are old enough now. And I don't think your parents know the full story either. Nor does Adam."

"No, I don't know what you're talking about," the forty-five-year-old said.

Greg offered the De Luze XO Fine Champagne cognac around before he sat back saying "Well, where shall we start?" He and Julia proceeded to recount their adventures in great detail, particularly the role that Nicholas Lebrecque and Anne, Greg's first wife had played. They recapped how they had all met, which Greg had talked about in *Twisted Reasons*: first Greg and Anne, then an Interpol agent, when they were hunting for Adam Kallay, Greg's best friend from college, who got involved in the first heist attempt. That's when they had all met Julia, who was Kallay's girlfriend at the time. Then how Julia and Anne had both been kidnapped by the 'merchants of evil' but had managed to escape or get rescued. And how Nicholas, who was a colleague of Anne's at Interpol, had always been supportive back-up as they fought the arms and human traffickers, and in fact had taken a leading role in finally defeating them.

They recounted how Anne, Greg's first wife — after whom Anne, their daughter and the children's mother, was named — was shot as they were stopping some terrorists from bringing enough nuclear material into the USA to blow up New York, Boston or Washington. And how Julia had in turn killed the main arms merchant, and how Greg had then taken care of her and eventually married her. And that Nicholas Labrecque was Greg's best man at their wedding. The kids just loved the entire story, which took a couple of hours after dinner, with the many side plots and questions that Lily and Andrew raised.

Finally, Anne looked at her phone and saw that it was well past midnight. "Andrew. Lily. It's time you went up to bed. I will be there too, soon, and I'll tuck you in. But say good night and Merry Christmas now to Grandma and Grandpa and to your dad and uncle before you go. Give everybody kisses. It was a wonderful Christmas, thank you."

Greg was ready to hit the sack as well, so when George and Anne went up to look after the children and turn in themselves a few minutes later, Julia was left alone with her son, Adam, who was still sipping on the cognac Greg had offered the adults to finish off the celebrations. She admired him from across the room: what an intelligent and handsome man he had turned into. But, like any mother, she worried that he had not yet found himself a partner.

For a fleeting second, Julia wondered whether she should tell him the truth: that he was, in fact, the son of Sergei Polyakov — who had violently raped both her and Anne, Greg's first wife and her friend. And the grandson of Lavrenti Beria, Stalin's perverted deputy[28], who had kidnapped and abused her aunt, along with countless other women. He would certainly know who Beria was, since he had majored in International Relations, with a special focus on Russian affairs at the Kennedy School, and now worked as a Russian expert at the State Department. She was proud that he had taken an interest in his heritage, and in fact, spoke the language fluently, although glad that, so far, the terrible truth had not come out.

And that is how it will remain, Julia told herself. *The secret will die with me.* No need to disrupt the life of this fine young man. The twisted fates of Adam, Greg, Anne, Polyakov, Hetzel and herself had already caused too much hurt and suffering, she told herself.

Julia stood up, went over to Adam and gave him a kiss on the forehead, saying, "Good night, my son. I am so glad to have you here with us." And she knew that he would not fully understand her meaning, but that was just a legacy of their twisted fates.

The End

Read the exciting 'Twisted' trilogy (or listen to all three books, now available as audiobooks on Amazon or Audible) to get the back story leading up to this Vermont Christmas episode.

Endnotes

[1] Deutschkreutz is the first village into Austria across from Kopháza in Hungary just south of the Neusiedler See, or Fertö Tó as it is known in Hungarian.

[2] I was raised as a Catholic.

[3] Under the Venice Protocol of October 13, 1921, Hungary, on the losing side in World War I, after the plebiscite, finally agreed to withdraw its troops from Burgenland – historically a part of Hungary – and cede it to Austria if, in return, it was granted the city of Sopron (Ödenburg).

[4] Gedeon Wein, my father's first cousin. "Bácsi" is the honorific used by children for older males, loosely translated as "Uncle".

[5] My parents had been planning to go with Gida bácsi to this first post-War soccer game between Austria and Hungary as a way of trying to get across to the part of Vienna under Allied control. However, on the way to the boat that would take them up the Danube, my mother's water broke (she was pregnant with my brother, Peter), and instead of trying to escape with Gida, they ended up going to the hospital for her to give birth.

[6] With cream, usually frothed.

[7] Pan-fried potatoes, similar to hashbrowns.

[8] The main shopping street of Vienna, leading from the Ring to the Stefansdom, or St. Stephen's Cathedral. This is the heart of the Imperial Capital.

[9] The Vienna State Opera House.

[10] This distant relative by marriage kindly took us in for most of our stay in Vienna after our escape. Alfred Jansa von Tannenau was a Field Marshall in the Austrian Army, and from 1936, its Chief of Staff. He is famous for developing the plans to defend Austria against a German attack, and as a known opponent of Hitler, was forced into exile in Erfurt

until the end of the war. He was a gentle and clever man, and my father was a particular favorite of his.

[11] A resort village on the north shore of Lake Balaton, where my paternal grandfather had a vacation house.

[12] A Viennese specialty, long cooked beef or veal in a broth.

[13] After my grandfather's death in 1953, my father had sent his mother – who, as a no longer productive senior, had no problems in getting the papers to leave Hungary – to join her two other children, Gabriel and Klára who were already in Canada. Part of the rationale for this was to make it easier for us to get in to Canada, since at the time Canadian immigration regulations required a vertical relationship (either parent or child, siblings not being good enough) to get into the country.

[14] A public educational institute and observatory built in 1909 right in the heart of Vienna.

[15] My maternal grandmother.

[16] The Imperial Palace right in the heart of Vienna.

[17] The main train station in Vienna at the time.

[18] The airport just outside Vienna, still very much in use today.

[19] Alfréd bácsi passed away on December 20, 1963, at age 79.

[20] One of Paris' many airports, still in use today especially for charter and low-cost flights.

[21] The name of the main town on the Island of Santa Maria in the Portuguese islands of the Azores.

[22] Forty-five years later, after the September 11, 2001, attacks, the generous people of Gander welcomed with similar kindness many passengers from planes forced to land there, as all flights to New York were being diverted. The wonderful Tony Award-winning Broadway musical, Come From Away, commemorates the true story of this event.

[23] The Toronto airport, named after the suburb Malton.

[24] My uncle had escaped at the end of the war. As a soldier in the Hungarian army, he was near the western front and Austria, and his

father-in-law got word to him that he should try to get across the demarcation line, because the Soviets were rounding up all males of military age and either executing them or sending them to gulags. He tied himself to the bottom of a train carriage until the first stop in Austria, where the station master at the first stop in Austria untied him and helped him. He was the first one in Canada and wrote glowing reports of life there to my parents

[25] My Aunt Klára had followed her younger brother to Canada, with her son and husband, settling in Montreal where he, as an aeronautical engineer and pilot, got a good job with Canadair.

[26] University of Western Ontario, in London, Ontario, where Peter was in his penultimate year. Sydenham Hall was Peter's dorm.

[27] A historical province of Finland, now divided between Finland and Russia.

About the Author

Born in Budapest, Geza Tatrallyay escaped with his family from Communist Hungary in 1956 during the Revolution, immigrating to Canada. After attending the University of Toronto Schools and serving as School Captain in his last year, he attended Harvard College, graduating in 1972 with a B.A. in Human Ecology, and, as a Rhodes Scholar from Ontario, obtained a B.A. / M.A. in Human Sciences from Oxford University in 1974. He completed his studies with a M.Sc. from London School of Economics and Politics in 1975. Geza worked as a host in the Ontario Pavilion at Expo '70, the world's fair in Osaka, Japan, and represented Canada in epée fencing at the Montreal Olympics in 1976, having won the National Championship that year. His professional experience has included stints in government, international finance and environmental entrepreneurship. Geza is a citizen of Canada and Hungary, and, as a green card holder, currently divides his time between Barnard, Vermont and San Francisco. He is married to Marcia Nousanen, and their daughter, Alexandra, lives in San Francisco with husband David, and two sons, Sebastian and Orlando, while their son, Nicholas, lives in Nairobi with his Hungarian wife, Fanni, and his granddaughters, Sophia and Lara. Geza is also the author of six novels, three memoirs, six poetry collections, a short story collection and a children's picture storybook published by different publishers in the USA, Canada and India. *Yuletide Jollies* will be his eighteenth book. His first murder mystery, *The Purple School Bus Murders,* soon-to-be-published, will be his nineteenth book and the first one in the genre. His poems, stories, essays and articles have been published in journals in Canada and the USA.

Other Books by Geza Tatrallyay

Arctic Meltdown, (thriller) 1st edition, e-published on Amazon and www.smashwords.com, December 2011

Twisted Reasons, (thriller, first book in 'Twisted' trilogy) November 2014, Deux Voiliers Publishing

Cello's Tears, (poetry collection) May 2015, P.R.A. Publishing

For the Children, (memoir) 1st edition, May 2015, Editions Dedicaces; revised 2nd edition and ebook published April 2024 by Ingram

The Expo Affair, (memoir) April 2016, Guernica Editions

Twisted Traffick, (thriller, second book in 'Twisted' trilogy) October 2017, Black Opal Books

Sighs and Murmurs, (poetry collection) April 2018, P.R.A. Publishing

Twisted Fates, (thriller, third book in 'Twisted' trilogy) June 2018, Black Opal Books

The Waffle and the Pancake, (children's picture storybook), September 2018, Bayeux Arts

The Rainbow Vintner, (thriller) February 2019, Black Opal Books

The Fencers, (memoir) March 2019, Deux Voiliers Publishing

Extinction, (poetry collection) April 2019, P.R.A. Publishing

Extinction Rebellion, (poetry collection) July 2020, Cyberwit

Arctic Meltdown, 2nd updated edition, (thriller), August 28, 2021, Black Opal Books

The Mind Spins, (short story collection), November 2021, P.R.A. Publishing *The Abyss: Poems for our World*, (poetry collection), September 2022, Deux Voiliers Publishing

Arctic Inferno, (thriller, sequel to *Arctic Meltdown*), August 2023, Black Opal Books

"Beastie" Poems, (poetry collection), December 2023, Cyberwit

www.ingramcontent.com/pod-product-compliance
Lightning Source LLC
LaVergne TN
LVHW091117150826
845673LV00002B/869

* 9 7 8 9 3 6 3 5 4 0 6 2 0 *